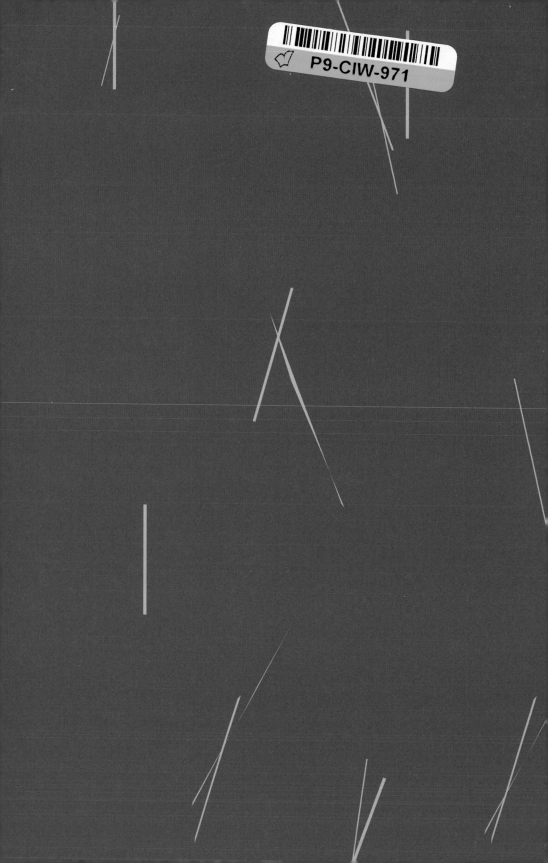

ALSO BY Robin Sharma

The Monk Who Sold His Ferrari

Leadership Wisdom from The Monk Who Sold His Ferrari

Family Wisdom from The Monk Who Sold His Ferrari

Who Will Cry When You Die?

MegaLiving

For more information on Robin Sharma's books,
audio programs, videos, and learning tools, please visit:
www.robinsharma.com

Please visit the Hay House Website
at **www.hayhouse.com**

THE SAINT THE SURFER AND THE CEO

A REMARKABLE STORY ABOUT LIVING YOUR HEART'S DESIRES

ROBIN SHARMA

HAY
HOUSE

Hay House, Inc.
Carlsbad, California • Sydney, Australia
Canada • Hong Kong • United Kingdom

Published and distributed in the United States by: Hay House, Inc., P.O. Box 5100, Carlsbad, CA 92018-5100 • (800) 654-5126 • (800) 650-5115 (fax) • www.hayhouse.com • *Published and distributed in Australia by:* Hay House Australia Pty Ltd, P.O. Box 515, Brighton-Le-Sands, NSW 2216 • *phone:* 1800 023 516 • *e-mail:* info@hayhouse.com.au • *Distributed in the United Kingdom by:* Airlift, 8 The Arena, Mollison Ave., Enfield, Middlesex, United Kingdom EN3 7NL • *Distributed in Canada by:* Raincoast, 9050 Shaughnessy St., Vancouver, B.C., Canada V6P 6E5

Editorial supervision: Jill Kramer • *Design:* Jenn Ramsey

Library of Congress Cataloging-in-Publication Data

Sharma, Robin S. (Robin Shilp)
   The saint, the surfer, and the CEO : a remarkable story about living your heart's desires / Robin Sharma.
      p. cm.
   ISBN 1-40190-016-X (hardcover) • ISBN 1-4019-0059-3 (Tradepapr)
   1. Self-actualization (Psychology)—Fiction. 2. Chief executive officers—Fiction. 3. Surfers—Fiction. 4. Saints—Fiction.
   I. Title.
PR9199.3.S497S25 2003
813'.54—dc21

                                                            2002009728

Hardcover ISBN 1-4019-0016-X
Tradepaper ISBN 1-4019-0059-3

05 04 03 02   4 3 2 1
1st printing, October 2002

Printed in the United States of America

To Jill Hewlett. I thank you for the magnificent growth you have inspired me to experience, and for the wonderful things you have taught me. I am grateful for your extraordinary support of me, my mission to make a difference in the world and for all of your love. You have blessed my life.

"Each man had only one genuine vocation—to find the way to himself. . . . His task was to discover his own destiny—not an arbitrary one—and live it out wholly and resolutely within himself. Everything else was only a would-be existence, an attempt at evasion, a flight back to the ideals of the masses, conformity and fear of one's own inwardness."

— from *Demian* by Hermann Hesse

"Perhaps love is the process of my leading you gently back to yourself. Not whom I want you to be, but to who you are."

— Antoine de Saint-Exupéry

CONTENTS

THE SAINT

THE SURFER

THE CEO

ACKNOWLEDGMENTS

I've been blessed to have an extraordinary support team of friends, family, and colleagues who have helped me on every step of the personal voyage I call a life. These people deserve deep thanks and real appreciation. And so I express all my gratitude to each and every one of them for assisting me as I walk the path of my personal mission.

A huge thank you goes to my team at Sharma Leadership International. I appreciate Ann Green, my kind and caring executive assistant and International Director of Client Relations, who has given me years of dedicated support and encouragement: You are wonderful. Thanks must also go to Marnie Ballane, our Vice President of Speaking Services & Learning Tools, who's a model of calm effectiveness and cheerful efficiency—I so value all that you bring to our enterprise. And to Al Moscardelli, our Senior Vice President and General Manager, you are brilliant at what you do and have helped us make a difference at a whole new level. You are all amazing human beings, and I love working with you.

Thanks to our corporate clients around the world for inviting me into your organizations as a leadership speaker, coach, and consultant. I'm grateful for the opportunity to be of service and add value. Thanks also to the individual clients whom I have the privilege to coach: You inspire me by your courage, and your dedication to exploring the frontiers of your best life. And to the clients who are members of my inner circle called *The Monthly Coach,* thank you for seeing the value in what I believe is to be a truly splendid vehicle to transform a life. Your success is my success.

To my agent, Ken Browning, you are a superstar, my friend. Thank you for quickly sensing my vision, seeing what I have to offer, and making things happen.

I acknowledge the wonderful support and work of the entire team at Hay House in California. I feel truly blessed to be one of your authors. I especially need to thank my editor, Jill Kramer, for always being there for me; Christy Salinas, for her very cool cover design; the PR team, for getting me out there; Reid Tracy, for believing in me; and Danny Levin, for his endless encouragement, excellent advice, and genuine friendship. This book reflects a team effort. I just happen to be the one who wrote the words.

Thanks must also go to our strategic partners worldwide who are helping me advance my mission to aid people in discovering who they truly are and transform employees into leaders. Special thanks to Tony Britt of The Britt Sales Corporation in New Jersey, Orit Valency in Israel, and our other affiliates.

Thanks to Diane Bliss and her fine team at PBS in Detroit for doing my television special and for assisting in spreading my message of life leadership. You've made a difference.

I also appreciate the contribution of Jonathan Creaghan in helping me get to a new understanding of "living in the possibility"; as well as those of Neil Parfitt, a truly gifted music composer, and Lyndsey Parfitt, an always energetic supporter.

I thank my colleagues John Gray, Mark Victor Hansen, Nido Qubein, Denis Waitley, and Wayne Dyer for being so very kind and giving. I appreciate all of the seminar promoters in both the United States and Canada who have sponsored me. Thanks especially to Salim Khoja and the exceptional team at 4 Walls in Toronto, Mike Walsh at High Performers International in Portland, Jeff Liesener at High Achievers Network in Phoenix, and the whole gang at Peak Performers in Minneapolis

I would not be the person I am without my friends, who have helped shape my thinking and supported my path. Special thanks to Richard Carlson, a man who is touching millions of lives and making the world a better place. Thanks to my mastermind partner Jeffrey Feldberg (a brilliant leader), Wayne Stark (a fearless visionary), Azim Jamal (a wise human being), Ernie Pavan (a talented guide), Kevin Higgins (a superb thinker), Darren and Lipi Bagshaw (genuinely caring change missionaries), Malcolm McKillop (a wonderful confidant), and Jerry Weiner (a much-valued mentor). Each one of you has made a significant contribution to my life. I thank you.

To my gifted brother, Dr. Sanjay Sharma—a powerhouse of ideas, creativity, and unconditional love—you have no idea how much I respect you. You and Susan, your equally remarkable and talented wife, are models to me of so many things. In my time of great need, you both stood with me, and for this I will be eternally grateful. Thanks also go to my nephew Neel for all the fun and playfulness.

I express my respect, love, and gratitude for my Mother Shashi and my Father Shiv. I owe so much to the both of you and acknowledge the gift of your guidance, kindness, and support. Please know that I recognize how much you both have done for me. It's been said that we choose our parents—one of my greatest gifts was in choosing the two of you.

Special thanks to Jill Hewlett for your extraordinary support, wisdom, and love.

And to my truly amazing children, Colby and Bianca (who provide me with endless joy and happiness), thanks from my heart for all the gifts you bring to me and for filling my life with a love that knows no bounds.

————— ◆ —————

INTRODUCTION

This book is a work of fiction. It's a story about a man named Jack Valentine, whose path in life was in many ways similar to my own. Feeling very incomplete as a human being, he set out on a search for wisdom to live a happier, healthier, and more beautiful life. Through a series of meetings with three remarkable teachers, Jack discovered a powerful philosophy to reshape his reality and access his destiny. The lessons Jack learned through his extraordinary adventure will cause you to create wonderful changes in your life as well. How do I know this? Because they're the lessons that have transformed *mine*.

I've experienced many setbacks along this journey through my days. And yet, each stumbling block has eventually presented a stepping-stone that has brought me closer to my heart's truth and my best life.

A number of years ago, I was a lawyer, chasing success and all the material trappings that went along with it, thinking that this was the way to lasting fulfillment. But as I worked harder and achieved more, I realized that nothing ever really changed. No matter how many material possessions I gathered, the man I saw in the bathroom mirror every morning was the same—I wasn't any happier and didn't feel any better. The more I reflected on the state of my life, I began to become aware of an emptiness within my heart. I started paying attention to its silent whispers, which instructed me to leave my chosen profession and begin some serious soul-searching. I started to think about why I was here on the planet and what my special mission was. I wondered why my life wasn't working and what deep changes needed to be made to get me on track. I looked at the core beliefs, assumptions, and filters through which I saw the world, and I committed myself to cleaning up the less-than-healthy ones.

During this time of intense transformation, I read books on self-help, personal leadership, philosophy, and spirituality. I took personal-development course after personal-development course. I changed my diet, my thinking, and my behaviors. Eventually, the person I evolved into was someone more authentic, harmonious, and wise than the person I once was.

I'll be the first to tell you that, in many ways, I'm still just a beginner on this journey of self-discovery. The top of one mountain is the bottom of the next for me, and my human exploration is a never-ending process. Even now, as I write these words, I'm moving through yet another period of massive personal transformation and reassessing my most fundamental values, along with the way I view the world. But I try to be gentle with myself. I remind myself that I must be patient and not "push the river." Each day brings greater clarity, more certainty, and new blessings. And to me, that's what this beautiful unfolding of life is all about.

I hope *The Saint, the Surfer, and the CEO* touches you at a deep level. If you really want to "own" this material, it's very important that you teach it. I suggest that within 24 hours of completing the book you sit down and share the philosophy you've learned with someone you care about. This will clarify your understanding and assist in integrating the lessons into your life.

I also hope that you have fun living the knowledge of this book. Bringing a childlike sense of wonder and passion to what you'll discover on the pages that follow is one of the best ways to grow into the person I know you're meant to become. Thank you for giving me the privilege of sharing this work with you. I wish for you a life rich with possibility, joy, and peace. And I hope that you'll do your part to help in the building of a new world.

— Robin Sharma

———— ✦ ————

1

> *"All of us, whether or not we are warriors, have a cubic centimeter of chance that pops out in front of our eyes from time to time. The difference between the average person and a warrior is that the warrior is aware of this and stays alert, deliberately waiting, so that when this cubic centimeter of chance pops out, it is picked up."*
>
> — Carlos Castaneda

———— ✦ ————

I had never felt so much pain in my life. My right hand was quivering uncontrollably, and blood was spilling all over my crisp white shirt. It was a Monday morning, and the only thought filling my head was that this was not a good day for me to die.

As I lay motionless in my car, I was struck by the silence of the scene. No one in the truck that had just crashed into me even so much as twitched. The onlookers who had gathered at the scene looked horrified. And traffic had come to a complete standstill. All I could hear were leaves rustling in the trees that lined the road next to me.

Two of the bystanders came running over, telling me that help was on the way and not to make any movements. One of them grasped my hand and started praying: "Lord, help this man. Please protect him." Within minutes, a cavalcade of ambulances, fire trucks, and police cruisers surrounded the accident scene with sirens blaring. Everything seemed to slow down, and a strange sense of peace passed through me as the rescue workers methodically began their work, shining examples of grace under pressure. I felt like a witness—almost as if I were watching the entire scene unfold from a high perch above.

The next thing I can recall is waking up in a hospital room that smelled like fresh lemons and bleach. I'll never forget that smell. My body was wrapped in various bandages, and both of my legs were in casts. My arms were covered with bruises.

I was greeted by a pretty young nurse. "Mr. Valentine! I can't believe you're awake! Let me call the doctor," she said while frantically dialing the intercom stationed next to my bed.

When she got off the intercom, I croaked out, "Call me Jack," attempting to be casual in what I knew was a serious situation. "Where am I?"

"You're at Lakeview General Hospital, Jack. This is the Critical Care ward. You had quite an accident last week. To be honest with you, you're very fortunate to be alive."

"I am?" I asked sheepishly.

"Un-huh," the nurse replied with a forced grin while she looked at the charts at the foot of my bed. "You fell into a coma after a pickup truck crashed into you. The paramedics who brought you in here couldn't believe you survived the crash. Anyway, the only thing you need to worry about now is healing those nasty wounds and your broken legs. You'll be just fine—as I said, you're an incredibly lucky young man."

Lucky was not a word I would have ever associated with

myself but, under the circumstances, I could see her point. I *was* blessed to be alive.

"Why am I all alone in this room?" I wondered aloud as I looked around. "I wouldn't mind some company."

"You've only been awake for a few minutes, Jack. Relax and give yourself some time to breathe. Be still. Your doctor will be here shortly—he was extremely worried about you."

—— ✦ ——

As the hours of that day passed and the barrage of doctors and nurses probed, checked, and encouraged me, I began to fully appreciate how serious my accident had been. The driver of the pickup truck had been killed instantly, and my doctor candidly informed me that he thought I'd never regain consciousness. "Never seen a case quite like this one," he stated matter-of-factly.

But I had a knowing within me that this had all happened for a reason. *Everything* happens for a reason, and there are no accidents in life—I know you've heard that before. But I've personally come to know that this breathtaking universe of ours is not only strikingly intelligent in its operation, it's also a very friendly place. This world wants us to live great lives. It wants us to be happy. And it wants us to win.

A quiet voice inside (which first appeared in that hospital room but would go on to comfort me during my most difficult and vulnerable times) informed me that something big was about to happen and that what I'd experience over the coming days and weeks would not only revolutionize my life, it would affect the lives of many others as well. It told me that my best was yet to come.

My guess is that many of us fail to listen to this quiet yet wise voice within us. There's a place deep inside every single one of our hearts that knows all the answers to our biggest questions. Each one of us knows our truth and what needs to be done to create extraordinary lives for ourselves. Most of us have simply lost the connection to this natural source of pure wisdom because too much noise and clutter dominates our days. But I've found that when I've made time for silence, stillness, and solitude, the voice of truth begins to speak. And the more I've trusted its guidance, the richer my life has become.

It was about 9:30 that night when an orderly wheeled another patient into my room. I was grateful for the company and immediately raised my head to catch a glimpse of my new companion. He was an elderly man, probably about 75 years of age. He had thick silver hair that was slicked back in a stylish way and brown spots over his face from what appeared to be many years of sun exposure. I detected from his frail appearance and his labored breathing that this man was quite ill. I also noted that he was in some pain—he kept his eyes closed and moaned softly as the orderly transferred him into his new bed.

After about ten minutes, the visitor slowly opened his eyes. I was spellbound: His eyes were dazzling blue and revealed a clarity and brilliance that sent a shiver up my spine. I immediately felt that the man before me had a depth of wisdom that was rare in this world of quick fixes and fast lives. I felt I was in the presence of a master.

"Good evening," he softly whispered in a dignified way. "Looks like we're in here together for a while."

"Yes—it's not the greatest place to spend a Friday night, is it?" I replied with a warm smile. "My name's Jack," I said, raising my hand as a greeting. "Jack Valentine. I was in a pretty serious car accident about a week ago, and the verdict is that I'll be in this bed for a while. I've felt alone all day, so I'm glad to meet you, sir."

"Good to meet you too, Jack. I'm Cal. I've been in this hospital, in various wards, for the past seven months. I've been tested, treated, and tracked more than I ever could have imagined. I'm afraid that the way things are going for me, I'm never going to get out of here," he offered quietly, his eyes darting up to the ceiling. He paused for a moment. "I came in here with a stomachache, which I thought was caused by something I ate. Six days later they had me in chemotherapy."

"Cancer?" I asked, trying to be as sensitive as possible.

"Yes. By the time the doctors detected it, they saw that it had spread throughout my body. It's in my lungs, it's in my gut, and it's now even in my head," he said as he shakily passed his right hand through his mop of hair. "Anyway," he continued in a reflective tone, "I've lived a pretty great life relative to most people. I grew up dirt poor, raised only by my mom. And what a noble woman she was."

"Same as mine," I interjected.

"I think about my mother every day," Cal replied. "She was sensitive, feisty, and strong as freshly forged steel. She believed in me like no one else I've ever met and encouraged me to set great goals and dream big dreams. Her love for me was truly unconditional—and that's the only kind of love that's real, Jack. Makes me think of what Victor Hugo once wrote: 'The supreme happiness of life is the conviction that we are loved.' And boy, did I feel loved by that extraordinary woman. You don't mind if I share my story with you, do you?"

"No, not at all," I replied. "Actually, I'm intrigued."

"Good. Well, my childhood was simple yet fun. Summers spent skinny-dipping at the swimming hole and winters spent in front of a roaring fire telling stories and reading great books.

My mom taught me to love books."

"I love books, too," I offered. "I really didn't enjoy school that much, but I cherished my books."

"I was a lot like that. As the great thinker Judah ibn-Tibbon observed so wisely: 'Make thy books thy companions. Let thy cases and shelves be thy pleasure grounds and gardens.'"

"Lovely words, Cal."

He continued. "School bored me, but I found great stimulation from books. I'll never forget my mother saying that one idea read in one book had the potential to transform my life. The real thing, she said, was that we just didn't know which book contained that one idea that would lead to our awakening! My duty, she would tell me with obvious love, was to keep searching for that book; once I found it, I had to have the personal courage to act on the idea so that results were brought into my life. Jack, since you love to read, too, I'll share a another quick quote on the power of reading with you."

"By all means."

"'The buying of more books than one can read is nothing less than the soul reaching toward infinity, and this passion is the only thing that raises us above the beasts that perish.' It's from A. Edward Norton—had to learn that one in high school," Cal mentioned as he repositioned himself in his bed.

"Anyway, once I got a little older, I went off to a military academy for further education and training. Mom never wanted me to leave, but I received a scholarship and it really was my ticket out of the poverty that I grew up in. After that, I went to college, and there, on my very first day on campus, I fell in love with an 18-year-old sweetie with golden hair and ivory skin. I met her in history class, and it truly was love at first sight. I just knew we were meant to be together. My God, I loved Grace—she was so innocent and kind. I couldn't have imagined a more splendid person for me to journey through life with."

"My mother's name was Grace, too," I remarked.

"Beautiful name, isn't it, Jack?"

"Yes, it is."

"After Grace and I were married, we had a child, a boy. I loved that kid so much. It was a very special time for us. We had fun, laughter, love—the best stuff of life. About that time I also decided to try my hand at business, starting a lumber concern that supplied many large contractors. It was during a time of great economic prosperity, and the construction boom was upon us. Over a period of years, I made a ton of money—millions of dollars, in fact—and the life that Grace, our son, and I began to lead was something right out of a storybook. Pure fantasy, I'd have to say," Cal noted, shaking his head as if he couldn't believe it himself.

"But, as I made more money, I became more consumed by work. I grew distracted and less attentive to my family. It's been said that as we move through life, we have to juggle a number of different balls. Some balls, like the one that represents career, are made of rubber. If we drop them, they have the ability to bounce back. But some balls are made of glass—family is like that. If you drop that ball, it doesn't come back. That's the mistake I made. Money just complicated things for me and sent me down the wrong path. I lost sight of my deepest values and my truest priorities. I moved farther away from my family rather than closer to them. The richest person in the world, I've since discovered, isn't the person who has the most but the one who needs the least. It took me a long time to get that lesson. And boy, did I pay a hefty price for it."

I listened intently, engrossed in the story of this man who was sharing his life's experiences so openly with me. I had also grown up without a father, so I was fascinated to hear Cal's

7

perspective on the importance of a strong family life. I longed for a connection to the father I never really knew and had always felt that a big piece of my life was missing because of this incompleteness. I also felt some sadness surfacing due to the fact that although I was a relatively young man, I still hadn't met a woman I felt I could share my life and start a family with. It was a longing I hadn't detected before.

"Anyway," Cal continued, his enthusiasm flowing, "hard times hit our industry, as they always do, and I lost every penny of my fortune. I'm not saying I lost *some* of the money and *some* of our belongings, Jack. I'm telling you that we lost it all in a matter of weeks. Grace took it very hard and worried endlessly about our dire straits. But we were strong people, and together we tried our best to rebuild.

"The business was scaled down considerably, and Grace and I retreated to a much simpler lifestyle. It was also a time of great internal reflection for the two of us. Failure often does that for people. It reawakens us to who we really are and to what we truly want, and it shakes us out of our complacency. And so, even though we were uncomfortable from an economic point of view and our relationship still faced its challenges, I grew immensely as a human being. In fact, the distress of that period started me on a path of self-discovery and personal growth that I still travel on this very day. It totally changed my life."

"So what happened next, Cal?" I asked with genuine interest, unconcerned that it was getting late and the lights in the hospital had all been turned off.

"I became a philosopher," came the straightforward reply.

"A philosopher? What about your business? And what about Grace and your son?"

"Philosophy simply means 'love of wisdom.' What I'm telling you, Jack, is that I came to love wisdom just as much as I loved life itself. I'd spend entire days pondering life's meaning and meditating on its deep issues. The things that I used to spend my days focusing on began to look trivial. Sadly, Grace and I began to drift apart even further and eventually we separated. Some people believe that relationships come to us as assignments. Some last for weeks, some for a lifetime—but they all come to teach us big lessons that are meant to spur our growth as people. All I know is that I learned so much from the time we had together. Unfortunately, she took our boy with her, and I never saw the two of them again. That crushed me," Cal said, his voice trembling. "A piece of me died when that happened. I still have trouble forgiving myself over what I did to destroy my family life. And God, how I missed that child.

"Last I heard, Grace moved across the country and tried to raise our son with the limited resources she had. I tried to remain in contact with her and help her out, but I knew her heart had been broken, and proud as she was, she'd have nothing to do with me. It truly was the greatest mistake of my life, losing my family. My wife and son brought me such extraordinarily happy moments, which I didn't see until it was too late. But our greatest mistakes also carry our largest lessons. I'm wiser now. I guess the real trick in life is to turn hindsight into foresight that reveals insight."

"Nice way to put it, Cal. What I really hear you saying is that it's important in life to let our past serve us. Is that right?"

"Very well put. That's it exactly. There's nothing wrong with making a mistake—that's how human beings grow. We're designed to make mistakes, for mistakes carry growth. We just shouldn't keep repeating the same one. Turn a wound into wisdom, or, as you said, let your past serve you.

"Anyway, after Grace and our son left, I, in turn, went even deeper into myself, closing myself off from the world for a period of years, and becoming deeply involved in self-examination and internal questioning. My passion became my quest to discover who I was as a human being and why my life had unfolded as it did. In a world where most people live on the outside, I lived within. In a world where people run away from their fears, I ran toward them. And what I saw within the deepest parts of me was incredible."

"Can you share what you saw within yourself?" I inquired eagerly, hanging on Cal's every word.

"I'll let you find that out for yourself, son," he replied, deepening my already burning sense of curiosity. "You know, we all have to do our own interior work. It's our highest responsibility. To examine yourself and get to know the real you—your true self—and all you are as a human being is the central aim of life. To know more about yourself so you can *be* more for the world is the ultimate journey. Genuine success in life is an inside job, you know."

"I understand completely."

"What I've found is that the best treasures a person will ever discover are those hidden within their heart. The greatest gifts of life are the inner gifts that are only revealed to those with the courage to look beyond the surface of their lives."

I thought about what he said for a moment. "Unfortunately, Cal, I've never been one for personal development. I work for an ad agency, so I spend my days in the corporate world. It's all about making money and looking good. I'm not proud of the way my world operates, but I've learned to play the game. And I play it fairly well. I've got a slick car, or at least I had one. I've got a hot apartment and cool friends. But at the end of the day, I still don't feel happy. Something's missing. I really get what you're saying about success being an inside job. If I felt good about myself, I know I'd feel a lot better about my life. So where could I start with this 'interior work,' as you call it?"

"You can begin by connecting to your mortality, Jack. Thinking about death is very life affirming, you know."

"Really?"

"Sure. It's only when we deeply and emotionally connect to the fact that our lives are short and our hours are limited that we can fully live, and give every bit of ourselves to our waking moments. If you had only one year left to live, I bet you'd live very differently than you do right now. You'd make certain that you lived without regrets; you'd take chances; you'd risk opening your heart for love; and you'd live with total passion, great gusto, and a lovely focus on the worthy."

"What do you mean by a 'focus on the worthy'?" I asked.

Cal slowly sat up and reached for the pencil that rested on the table beside him.

"Live like this pencil and you'll have a fine life," he offered in a confident tone. "Too many of us live our lives like a rounded edge. We need to sharpen our focus and live to the point—just like a pencil. This is how you design and then build an extraordinary experience of life for yourself. The writer Michel Eyquem de Montaigne put it this way: 'The great and glorious masterpiece of human beings is to live to the point. All other things are at most but inconsiderable props and appendages.' You see, Jack, most of us live our lives as if we had all the time in the world. We deny ourselves our passions and we postpone our dreams. But life really is a fragile gift, and it needs to be lived right now. Neither of us knows how many tomorrows we have left. Please trust me on this one."

"I will," I said sincerely, sensing how important this lesson was for my new friend.

"Focus on the things that truly count in your life. Now that I'm older and wiser, I've discovered that the things I once believed to be the big things in life are actually the little things. And all those things that I believed to be the little, insignificant things early on have turned out to be the big things—the things that actually matter the most."

"And how would I go about connecting to my mortality?"

"Ask yourself The Final Questions," came the clear reply.

"The Final Questions? I'm not familiar with these, Cal. What are you talking about?" I sat up in my bed, completely transfixed by what I was hearing from this unique and somewhat mysterious man.

"When you lie on your deathbed taking your last breaths, there will be only three questions that will be at the forefront of your mind. These are what I call a person's Final Questions. And since they'll be the most important considerations at the end of your life, why not exercise the personal bravery to make them your most important considerations today."

"And the questions are?" I asked, sensing that what I was about to hear just might change my life.

"They're simply: *'Did I live wisely?' 'Did I love well?'* and *'Did I serve greatly?'*"

"Could you please explain each of these?" I asked eagerly. "I know it's late, but this information could really change everything for me."

"Jack, even though I need to get some sleep, I appreciate your enthusiasm. There's no doubt in my mind that you and I have been brought together for a reason. That's just the way the world works. Everyone who enters your life comes to you at precisely the time that you most need to learn the lesson they've come to teach."

"I believe that."

"Our world is a very wise place, and our lives unfold according to a series of natural laws that are nothing less than brilliant.

We human beings think that our lives are governed by random events and that the people who enter and exit do so purely by chance. Nothing could be further from the truth. There's no chaos in our world, only order. There are no coincidences—*ever.* Our lives aren't run by good or bad luck, but by an intelligent process designed to help us evolve into our best selves."

"How do you know this?"

"I just know. And so will you," Cal stated with certainty.

"Interesting," I replied, deep in thought.

"You were born to present your gifts to the world. But the way it's set up is that before you can shine as a person—and I mean really shine—you must do that interior work I spoke of earlier. You must get to know yourself; you must look at your limiting beliefs and recreate them. And you must analyze the false assumptions you have about what you can be, have, and do as a person and then set about correcting them. You need to become aware of your historical patterns of reacting in the different scenarios of your life and re-create them. And you must tackle your fears and move through them. Then you can open up your heart and be more concerned about the happiness of other people than about the happiness of yourself. And once you do, ironically, you'll become happy."

"So it's all set up in a very methodical way," I said, summarizing the knowledge I'd just been exposed to. "The world has a grand design and order to it. I guess the first thing I must do is understand the natural laws it's governed by?"

"Yes, son," Cal replied, clearly pleased by my openness to his philosophy on life. "Once you align yourself with these laws, you'll access your authentic power. You'll become a force of nature, and your life will move from a place of struggle into one of ease and flow. All that you've ever dreamed of being you will become. You'll naturally draw into your life all that your heart has ever desired without effort. Your life will begin, to work, almost as if guided by magic."

I absorbed what he said for a moment, and then said, "I'm wondering exactly where I should start, though. I'll confess that this is a time of genuine struggle for me. I don't really know who I am anymore, and I'm just itching to make my life better. I recently ended my relationship with my girlfriend. I can't stand my job. I never have much money at the end of the month, even though I make a good salary. And I seem to have this deep ache within me that never leaves."

"Trust that ache, son."

"What?" I asked, unsure that I'd heard him correctly.

"Trust that ache," Cal repeated. "I've learned from my teachers that only when we go into the feelings and longings that most of us run away from will we find our greatest answers. Our feelings grant us immense wisdom and carry the knowledge of our subconscious minds. And our subconscious minds are our link to the wisdom of the universe. Our conscious thinking is so limited, but our subconscious thinking is infinite.

"You know, most of us deny our feelings. Society has taught us to do that. From a young age, we divorce ourselves from the way we feel. We're told not to cry, we're told not to laugh too loud, and we're told that it's wrong to feel sad or even to experience our anger. But our feelings are neither right nor wrong— they're simply our feelings, and an essential part of the human experience. Deny them and you begin to shut down parts of yourself. Keep doing that and you'll lose the connection to who you truly are. You'll begin living completely in your head, and you'll stop feeling."

Cal stopped for a moment and looked me in the eye. "I'd be willing to bet, Jack, that all you do, all day long, is think, think, think. Your mind is a nonstop chattering machine, and you have no inner peace. You've stopped living in the present moment and *feeling* what it's like to be fully alive—you're too busy living in the past or in the future. Did you know that the mind rarely lives in the present moment? It's always worrying about the past or thinking about the future. But that stuff isn't real. All that's real is the moment right in front of you. Don't miss that moment, because that's where your life is."

"So true," I remarked, letting out a deep sigh. This man's words reflected the truth—I felt it in my body. "This is all starting to make perfect sense," I noted. "I wish more people would hear the wisdom you're sharing with me and open up their eyes to it. The world would be a better place."

"They'll get it when they're ready to get it. As the old saying goes, 'When the student is ready, the teacher appears.' You can't push the river, you know."

"I guess there's just too much cynicism in the world today," I answered. "We don't believe in the great dreams we had as kids anymore. We don't believe we have the power to create the lives we want. We don't think that we can really make a difference by the things we do."

Cal nodded. "And that's exactly why so many of us are stuck. We have phenomenal power within us; we've just lost our connection to it. Part of the reason for this is fear. The possibilities available to us in our lives are truly miraculous. The wonders we have the potential to create in our lives, once we align with the force of nature, are astounding—they really are. But all this potential also brings with it certain responsibilities . . . and this frightens us. So we don't believe in ourselves. We deny our power and set up blocks to the achievement of the extraordinary lives that we're meant to lead."

"It's almost like we sabotage ourselves. We run away from the very thing we want the most."

"That's exactly what we do. We pretend we don't matter, and we act as if we're not special. We close our eyes to the way the world really operates, so we don't trust in these natural laws that govern it. And these laws only come alive in your life once you invest every bit of the trust you have as a human being in them. *They don't work if you don't believe they will work.* To access our best lives, each and every one of us must make some fundamental shifts of the mind. Maybe even more important, we each must make some fundamental shifts of the heart. And that begins by trusting these laws of nature I've been telling you about."

"So first I should *trust* that these laws work—and then they will?"

"Correct. It's set up a little like a fireplace. You need to put the logs in before you get the heat. Sitting in front of a logless fireplace just doesn't get you any warmer. Most people don't trust—they have no faith in the brilliance of the universe and their lovely role within it. That's why there's no magic in their lives. It's because they fail to understand the way the world operates, and it's also because they're no longer leaders."

I was puzzled by that remark. "What do you mean by that?"

"The starting point of enlightenment, a goal that every person should strive for, is inner leadership. Leadership is far more than something businesspeople do at work. Leadership is all about personal responsibility, self-discovery, and creating value in the world by the people we become. Too many people spend their time blaming others for all that isn't working in their lives. We blame our spouses for our unhappy home lives; we blame our bosses for our distress at work; we blame strangers on the freeway for making us angry; we blame our parents for keeping us small. Blame, blame, blame, blame. But blaming others is nothing more than excusing yourself. Blaming others for the current quality of your life is a sad way to live. In doing so, all you're doing is playing the victim."

"Really?"

"Definitely. Because, in living like that, what you're essentially saying is that you're powerless to lead your life. What you're saying is for your life to change, your spouse must change or your boss must change or the strangers on the freeway must change. That's a very impotent way to live. Where's the leadership in that philosophy of life?" Cal observed, his voice growing louder as his intensity increased. "The only way to lift your life to the next level is to act like a leader and assume real leadership over your life. The moment you look in the mirror and say to yourself, from the deepest place within you, 'For my life to change, *I* must change'—that's the moment you'll grow up and walk through a doorway that will lead you to your best life."

"Why is that so, I wonder?"

"Because, Jack, that's when you'll take your life into your own hands," Cal said passionately as he raised his hands into the air with dramatic flair. "You'll assume responsibility for the destiny that has been presented to you. You'll stop *resisting* your life and accept what is. You'll align yourself with those immutable laws of nature that I've been sharing with you, laws that have always governed the way the life works, from the beginning of time. *You'll get your power back.*"

Cal stopped and looked deep into my eyes. "Point your index finger at me, son," he said.

"What?"

"Just do it," he replied firmly.

I raised my hand and pointed directly at my uniquely eccentric roommate.

"What do you notice?" he quizzed.

"My skin seems to be peeling," I replied honestly.

"No, son. Think more deeply, which is something we all need to do more of as we journey through life. Reflection is the mother of wisdom, you know. Okay, so you have one finger pointing at me, but who are the other fingers pointing toward?"

I was struck by Cal's simple yet powerful demonstration. His point was clear: for every finger we point at another, we have three pointing back at us. I shared this realization with him.

"Now you're getting it!" he exclaimed joyfully. "Stop blaming others for everything you dislike about your life. Look in the mirror and regain some accountability over your life. That's how personal change and life leadership begins."

I smiled at him. "Okay, I see where you're coming from." I took a moment to let Cal's wisdom and lessons integrate. Then I said, "You don't think like most people."

"I know. That's because I see more than most people. And it's not because I'm better than anyone else—it's because I've been taught by the best," Cal responded humbly.

"What do you mean by that?"

"Well, it makes me think of what the father of classical physics, Isaac Newton, said: 'If I have seen farther than others, it is because I have stood on the shoulders of giants.' You see, I've been blessed by having some extraordinary guides in my life. The wisdom I'm sharing with you isn't mine."

"It's not?"

"No, not really. I learned it from my three teachers, three extraordinary human beings that transformed my life. I owe everything to them."

"Can I meet them?" I asked excitedly.

"Of course you can—sooner than you think, actually. They'll be the ones to explain to you the meaning of the Final Questions I alluded to earlier. They'll be the ones to really give you the answers you're looking for. They're the best resources I know of on what it means to be a true leader of your life and live congruently with the natural laws of the world. *They're* the masters. I'm only the student."

Just then, Cal began to cough. It started off in a mild way but quickly grew acute. His face became red, and a line of sweat drizzled down his forehead.

"My God, Cal! Should I call the nurse?" I asked with concern.

"No, I'll be okay," he replied, wheezing and looking deathly pale. "I really think I need to get some sleep now. I promise that tomorrow will be a very big day for you—it may even be your biggest day yet. It just might be your new beginning," he added with suspense, his blue eyes sparkling like stars on a cold winter's night.

"It's been really great meeting you, Jack," Cal continued. "As I say, *it was meant to be,* this beautiful connection we've made. We entered each other's lives tonight for a reason. *That's just the way the world works,*" he said with a smile as he rolled over and pulled the covers over his shoulders, chuckling to himself. "That's just the way the world works," he repeated. "Life truly is beautiful."

The room was silent for a moment.

"Oh, and by the way, son," he added gently, "I love you."

———— ✦ ————

2 GETTING ONTO THE PATH

"To live in hearts we leave behind is not to die."

— Thomas Campbell

——— ✦ ———

I awoke the next morning with bright sunlight streaming onto my face. I felt much better, and although I knew it would be a while before I would be completely recovered, I had a newfound sense of hope. I realized that, no matter what happened, I'd be okay.

The conversation I'd had the previous night with Cal— a most unique and intriguing man—had left me feeling a joy that I hadn't experienced in years. His wisdom and philosophy about the way our lives unfold was nothing short of remarkable. And I couldn't wait for him to introduce me to the three teachers who had transformed his life.

Although I thought it was odd that he'd told me he loved me as he drifted off to sleep, I assumed it was simply another of his practices for living a richer life and showing authentic leadership. I couldn't wait to continue our dialogue and learn more from this man I'd quickly developed a deep respect for.

"Good morning, Cal," I said enthusiastically as I stretched

like a cat in my standard-issue hospital bed. "This is going to be a great day for us, my friend."

Cal was facing the other direction and did not respond.

"Hey Cal, it's already ten o'clock—time to wake up. Don't make me come over there and get you," I offered playfully.

But Cal didn't move. A cramp quickly knotted my gut, my head started to spin, and I feared the worst. "Nurse!" I yelled. "Please, I need some help fast!"

Three nurses sprinted into the room.

"I think something's wrong with Cal! He was okay last night until he started to cough. He told me he'd be okay, but now it doesn't seem that he is."

Cal remained still as the nurses tended to him.

"I really hope he's okay," I said, filled with worry.

"Cal's dead," the most senior of the three nurses stated. "I'm sorry," she added with a little more gentleness.

"Cal's been very sick for a very long time, Jack," remarked another of the nurses. "His cancer had spread through his body, and we just couldn't do anything for him. He specifically asked to be brought up here last night—none of us really knew why. It was his final request. And we were more than happy to comply with it."

"He just said he knew you from a long time ago and he wanted to meet you," the senior nurse stated. "Cal was always a pretty mysterious man, you know."

"I know," I replied. I felt true sadness in my heart over the loss of a person I knew had come into my life as an angel of sorts, guiding my life into a new direction and offering me the new beginning that I'd so longed for.

"Cal was an amazing man," I said with respect. "I can't believe he's dead—in a short time he changed me in a way I've yet to fully appreciate."

"That's just the way the world works," all three nurses said in unison, using one of the pet phrases of my departed roommate. They smiled at each other.

"We loved Cal," one of them offered. "By the way," she added as the other two covered Cal's face with a sheet and tenderly wheeled him out of the room, "he left a package for you. We were instructed to give it to you this morning. It was almost as if he knew he would die last night," she said softly, tears welling up in her eyes. "Let me get it for you."

Within minutes the nurse returned. She passed me the package, which was covered with ornate wrapping paper that depicted little children swimming and frolicking in the sand. These images had been expertly drawn by hand and colored with crayons. And they were fantastic.

"Would you mind if I open this alone?" I asked the nurse. "I just feel that this is a personal moment for me, and I'd like to experience it by myself. It'll be my way of honoring Cal."

"Of course. No sweat," she replied. "We're all very sad about Cal, but just let us know if there's anything we can do for you. We'll just be down the hallway at the nurses' station."

"Thanks."

I carefully unwrapped the package. I had to remove several layers of tissue paper to get to the gift within. And once I reached it, I was astonished by what I saw.

Neatly placed, one on top of another, were three airline tickets. As I looked more closely, I saw that they were first-class passages to three of the most remarkable places in the world: Rome, Hawaii, and New York City.

Along with the plane tickets was a map of each destination, with directions scrawled in red ink and an "x" with a circle around it, showing the location I assumed I was to reach. The final element of this gift was a handwritten note from Cal. It read:

Dear Jack,

Sorry to leave you so quickly, son. I knew I'd go soon. You're a fine young man with great potential, and I know that you're destined for a life of honor, joy, and beautiful growth. I leave you not feeling sad but immensely happy and fulfilled. You see, I've lived a great life, enjoying more than my fair share of celebrations under the stars and special moments under the sun.

I've traveled down through life's valleys and experienced deep sadness. And I've journeyed high along its peaks, feeling more happiness than I've had any right to. Yes, I've made more than my share of mistakes. But son, I'm a practical man—always have been. So I've learned that it's better to risk and fail than to not risk at all.

I know that you're at a crossroads in your life right now. While this might seem like a difficult time, as you seek the answers to your largest questions, know that it's also a wonderful time. Human beings are most alive when living in the unknown, for it's in this place where anything and everything is possible. You're opening up to the world, and so the world will now begin to open up to you.

I cannot teach you all that you need to learn. While I've grown wiser along the path of my life, there are other teachers whose feet you need to sit at and whose powerful wisdom you need to learn from: three in particular. And as soon as you fully recover, I urge you to visit them. They're honorable, giving people. They each have discovered how to create an extraordinary life. And they've agreed to be your guides.

I've provided you with three plane tickets. First, go to Rome. Follow the directions on the map and meet your first teacher. It's all been arranged. Once there, you'll learn about the first of The Final Questions: "Have I lived wisely?" You'll find out how to conduct your life so that it's lived in a noble and enlightened way. From this first teacher, you'll learn the importance of discovering the gifts on the inside of your life so you can live with immense peace on the outside. You'll discover how to go deep as a person.

Then travel to Hawaii. The guide you'll meet there is quite a charac-
ter. But don't be deceived by his simple appearance and playful behavior.
This teacher is a genuine master. He'll explain a splendid philosophy around
the second of the Final Questions: "Have I loved well?" With him you'll
learn how to love life itself and each of the moments that occur within it.
He'll inspire you to experience your bliss, live with a wonderful sense of
adventure, and open your heart to an entirely new reality.

And then, to complete your personal transformation, you'll journey to
New York City. There you'll meet a truly exceptional human being who
will take you through the third of the Final Questions: "Have I served great-
ly?" With this teacher, you'll be shown how to be a leader on the planet, not
only in terms of your career but also in terms of your life.

This entire process will take you three months, but I promise that
you'll fundamentally change as a result of it. How do I know this? Because
I changed at a core level as a result of what they taught me. Please don't let
the inner critic that might be starting to awaken in your mind at this
moment take over. This gremlin always starts to chatter when we're pre-
sented with an opportunity to grow as people. It's nothing more than the
voice of fear. And it isn't your truth speaking. It isn't you. Simply trust in the
process I'm lovingly offering to you. Release any concerns that you have
about this path you're about to walk on, and just go into it with the curiosi-
ty of a child, knowing that you'll come out on the other side as a new person,
or to be more accurate, far more of the person who you truly are and have
been created to be.

I wish I could guide you through all this, but this is a solitary journey
that you alone must take. So I wish you well, son. I bless your life. I pray
for your success. And I give you all my love.

Your father,
Cal Valentine

I was astonished by this note, especially the way it ended. Could Cal have really been the father I never knew? Many questions remained unanswered as a barrage of thoughts rippled through my mind. *Where had he been all these years? Why hadn't he tried to contact me? Why didn't he tell me who he was in his remaining moments? Should I feel love for him, or anger over the fact that he'd abandoned my mother and me so many years ago?* I was completely confused. And I felt all my ancient wounds opening up again. I then looked down at the package, wondering whether the plane tickets were real and if the instructions Cal had provided could be trusted. Would this journey he recommended be safe?

But then something within me began to shift. Cal had been so very kind to me during our brief time together. I sensed that all he wanted to do in his last hours on Earth was to help me, guide me, and teach me. I felt his love and I knew it was true. His wish was for me to take this trip, and I felt compelled to do so. I'd deal with my hurt as the days went by—but I knew I'd be just fine.

As I sat alone in my hospital bed, one word dominated my consciousness at that time: *trust*. And so I did. I didn't have to figure everything out right this second. My life was opening up, and I was just going to enjoy the ride. I'd spent far too much time trying to work it all out in the past—planning, thinking, and worrying. The world had presented me with a glorious opportunity, and I felt free to seize it. I told myself that if figuring things out in my head was the way to find the answers I needed to create the extraordinary life I'd always wanted, then I'd have those answers by now.

A voice within me said, "There's another way to live, Jack. And it's a far more powerful way to operate. It has nothing to do with figuring things out in your head—it has everything to do with listening to the whispers of the heart. Stop being so busy *doing* and begin to spend more time just *being.* Set an intention to align your life with the natural power that runs the world. It's there that your answers lie."

I once read a quote from the respected psychologist Abraham Maslow that has never left me. His words were most appropriate for the journey I was about to embark upon. I'd like to share them with you:

> *"We fear our highest possibilities. . . . We are generally afraid to become that which we can glimpse in our most perfect moments, under the most perfect conditions, under times of great courage. We enjoy and even thrill in the possibilities we see in ourselves in such peak moments and yet we simultaneously shiver with weakness, awe, and fear before these very same possibilities."*

As I closed my eyes, I felt the sunlight on my face and the rhythmic beating of my heart. I had a knowing inside the core of my being that my life—my best life—was moving toward me. I felt my destiny coming to get me.

——— ◆ ———

3 OPENING UP TO THE WAY THE WORLD REALLY WORKS

"*Those who live nobly, even if in their life they live obscurely, need not fear that they will have lived in vain. Something radiates from their lives, some light that shows the way to their friends, their neighbors, perhaps to long future ages.*"

— Bertrand Russell

"*Remember who you are, she said. You're a master.*"

— Aniesa Thames

— ◆ —

It was springtime, and I was in Rome. It was a beautiful time to be alive. I'd recovered completely from the accident and had never felt better. I'd taken a three-month sabbatical from my position at the advertising agency and had rented my apartment to an old college friend who couldn't have been happier with her good fortune. I gained completion in the relationship with my former girlfriend, and I'm happy to say that we parted as friends. I was feeling good about my life for the first time in years. And I was ready for an adventure.

The experience I'd had with Cal never left my mind. Ever since our magical meeting, not one day had passed when I didn't think about him and his wisdom for at least a few moments. His knowledge had sunk deep to my roots, and I'd gained fresh insights on his unique perspectives each and every day since his passing. And I discovered that he proved to be completely worthy of my trust: The first-class ticket to Rome was legitimate, and as he promised, everything about the trip had been arranged splendidly. Cal had clearly given a lot of thought to my personal transformation and had put great care in getting all the details of this unique voyage just right. I could feel his love for me right now.

I can't believe it—here I am in Rome, with all the time in the world, and nothing but a backpack with a few items of clothing in it to worry about, I thought as I strolled along the narrow cobblestone streets in the older section of the city. There was a sweet smell in the air that made me smile and relax amidst this new environment. I felt as if I were *meant* to be in this incredible place, where my journey of self-discovery was set to begin. It was almost as if fate had attracted Cal into my life, and destiny had led me to where I stood now. All I could do was stay fully present in the moment and open up to whatever was meant to unfold for me. This was a completely different modus operandi for me, a far cry from the planned and rigid lifestyle that had characterized my days up until the car accident.

And yet, a part of me knew that this new way to be was far more powerful than the old one. My life now seemed to be leading me, and I was ready to enjoy the gifts and savor the surprises. To be even more specific, it was almost as if a set of hidden hands or an invisible force was guiding me in the direction of my highest and most authentic life. It really is hard to explain how this all felt at this time of my life. But I will say that I felt completely at ease and profoundly at peace.

I've since come to understand that this force, this invisible power, is the force of nature. It's the same power that created the stars and gives rise to the sunset. It pulses through every living being and is available to anyone with the awareness to detect it and then align themselves with it.

It all begins with a commitment to remove the blinders that most of us have placed upon our worldview and seek out the truth. And the truth became clearer to me as I went deeper into myself. I believe that's what real leadership as a human being is all about. It's nothing more than an individual quest for the truth—the truth about what we've experienced in the past and what we can become in our future; the truth about why we're here and how we got to where we are. Discovering the truth and then leading our lives by it is what sets us free.

Through my experiences and personal lessons along the way, I've learned that leadership of my life is also about releasing the tight grasp I've kept on my current reality. We all need to dispense with this addiction so many of us have to knowing how our lives are meant to turn out in advance. The fact of the matter is that we grow into our most powerful selves (or at least start the process) the moment we let go of all the control we so fearfully cling to, and open ourselves up to all possibilities that this glorious universe of ours presents. This is a great act of humility because it requires us to let go of the belief that *we* know what's best for us. It requires us to realize that what we think is needed in our lives to make us happy might not be what we need at all. And I say that this release of control is a great act of humility because it really does insist that we surrender ourselves to the much more powerful intelligence of the world we live in. I know it's scary stuff at first, but I've found that on the other side of our biggest fears resides our greatest fortune.

I guess it's all about having the faith that even if our lives don't unfold according to our best-laid plans, they're going to turn out just fine. And it's all about believing in a higher success well beyond the scope of what we can currently see. Arthur Shopenhauer almost had it when he observed: "Every man takes the limits of his own field of vision for the limits of the world." But a few do not. Join them.

— ✦ —

I'd been following Cal's directions for about an hour when I drew near to the place marked on the map with an "x." His handwritten scrawl stated cryptically: "Find the stained glass window and you'll see the world through new lenses." As I continued up the road, looking for the building marked on the map, I saw something that took my breath away.

Directly in front of me was an incredibly beautiful cathedral, with its doors wide open and bouquets of roses lining the steps. Baroque music spilled out of its entrance, and splendid sounds poured out into the street. Stone markings covered the pillars that stood at its front and, sure enough, standing proud and tall at the center of it all was the most spectacular stained glass window I'd ever seen.

I just stood there in awe, listening to the music and soaking up the brilliance of the moment. Tears actually began to form in my eyes, my heartbeat started to quicken, and my palms started to sweat. Our lives, I've realized, are nothing more than a series of moments—if you miss the moments, you miss your life. Thankfully, I had the wisdom to enjoy that special moment, which in some way connected me to something larger than myself. The feeling I had reminded me that I wasn't alone, and that I never had been throughout my life. It reminded me of the famous "Footprints" story written by Margaret Fishback Powers, in which a man had a dream that he saw himself walking on a beach alongside God. Across the sky flashed various scenes from this man's life, and for each scene, the man could see two sets of footprints in the sand. One set was his own and the other belonged to God.

Suddenly the man noticed something fascinating as he surveyed all the scenes of his existence: During certain times, there was only one set of footprints in the sand. And this single set of footprints only appeared during the most difficult and painful times of his life's journey. So the man confronted God with this observation, expressing his disappointment that he was left alone when he most needed help. God lovingly explained that during the painful times, he *carried* the man.

I was thinking about this very special dream that changed the way the man viewed the world when a powerful voice bellowed from inside of the cathedral: "Jack, you made it! Great to see you here!"

A priest came running out to greet me. He was dressed in his traditional clothing of worship, with a rosary in one hand and a book tied with a bright red bow in the other. He sauntered down the steps and stopped directly in front of me, grinning.

"This is for you, Jack," he said as he handed me the book. "Cal told me you'd be coming. We're all set up for your stay. I hope you enjoy this gift—it's a journal for you to record your insights in. Journaling is a powerful practice for self-change, and I know that you'll have many observations to note over the course of your stay here."

"My stay?"

"Yes, my young friend. You'll be with me here at the cathedral for the next four weeks. I'll be your life coach, helping you access your highest and best self. I'll teach you about things such as destiny, authenticity, and integrity. I'll show you how to access your true power, and I'll get you to your spirit. We'll have a *great* time together!" he exclaimed energetically.

"Thanks—but to be honest, I'm not really a religious person," I admitted frankly.

"What I have to teach you has nothing to do with religion. Being a spiritual human being is really about being an *authentic* human being. It's about living under your noblest personal values, being true in the way you conduct your life, and seeing the world in a more evolved and enlightened way."

"Okay, I'm definitely into that," I replied, placing my knapsack on the ground and taking a sip from my water bottle. "I couldn't be more ready for changes in my life."

"Perfect. Cal asked me to arrange everything for you, and I gladly obliged. I'm going to teach you about the meaning of life. I'll explain exactly how to awaken your highest talents, how to access your deepest wisdom, and how to leave a legacy. Basically, I'll show you how to live with wisdom—how to live a wise life."

"The first of the Final Questions," I noted, remembering the three important questions of life that Cal had explained to me during our unforgettable night in the hospital.

"Yes. I'll see to it that when the time eventually comes for you to ask yourself, 'Have I lived wisely?' your answer will be, 'Absolutely!' I want you to live so wisely that you'll die happily. Welcome to Roma!" he yelled with all the emotion and enthusiasm of an Italian opera star. "Forgive me for not introducing myself—I'm Father Michael Antonio Di Franco. My friends call me Father Mike," he said with a wink.

"Great to meet you, Father Mike. I appreciate your warm welcome," I stated sincerely, feeling completely comfortable in the company of this small man with the round face and slicked-back hair. "You knew Cal?"

"Oh, yes. Your father was a great man, Jack. A very special human being in so many ways. He told me all about you. Even though you're a grown man now, you still look much like the young boy in the photo he used to carry around with him. That's why it was easy for me to recognize you today."

"I still find it unbelievable that Cal was my father. Do you know why he left my mom and me? Why didn't he ever try to contact me? If the man was my father, you'd think he would have tried to find me," I said with anger welling up within me. "Fathers just don't forget about their kids."

"I don't know a lot about what caused your parents to separate. All he told me was that he and your mother drifted apart after his business fell on difficult times. The sense I get is that your father began to go inward after he lost his fortune, and the way he experienced the world began to shift. I think a time came when the two of them just realized that they were moving in different directions as people. Cal told me that he still loved your mother, but I guess they just decided they had to move on. I can't imagine how painful that must have been for you, Jack. But you should know that your father was a very loving man. He really cared immensely about people—and he cared the most about you."

"Thanks for telling me that," I said quietly. I'd spent so many sleepless nights as a child wondering about my father. He'd missed my Christmas concerts, my school plays, and my soccer games . . . I felt some solace in knowing that he really did love me.

"Your father nicknamed me 'The Saint' because I've devoted my life to living in a very noble, wise, and authentic way. He came to me many years earlier to learn the very lessons you'll soon discover. Cal was a philosopher in the truest sense of the word. He loved to learn and was very committed to deepening himself. And as far as I'm concerned, that's the best thing a human being can do. Did you know that he took the very journey that you've now embarked on? Like father, like son," he chuckled. "Anyway, I'm so happy that you're finally here."

"I'm really excited to be here, too, Father Mike. But to be honest, I'm a little unsure about all of this. Actually, I'll admit I'm feeling nervous. This has all been a lot to take in a short period of time."

"I hear you, Jack. I hear you completely. You're about to learn something new, so it's natural that your fears are starting to come up, manifesting themselves as this uncertainty and nervousness. But you must trust—after all, isn't it all about trust? Trust that Cal appeared when you most needed to meet him. Trust that you and I have connected for a special reason. Trust that there's no better place for you to be than where you are now. And trust that the next four weeks with me will reveal an entirely new way of thinking and being. We can change the way we see the world in an instant, you know. One single shift that takes place in a single second just might be all it takes to awaken a new reality for you."

"So you're one of the great teachers that my father spoke of?" I asked as he put his arm around me and walked me up the stone steps of the cathedral.

"Yes, that's correct. Your dad really was a wonderful man. I know he made mistakes in his life, such as not knowing you and showing you his love, but I've yet to meet a perfect human being. The very condition of the human being is one of imperfection, yet I've come to understand that we're actually perfect in our imperfection. If we didn't have our weaknesses, we'd have nothing to work on as we journeyed through life. As the mystics have said: 'The path has no value when you have arrived.' Our less-than-ideal traits are actually precious treasures that offer gateways into higher versions of the people that we currently are."

This last point intrigued me. Could Father Mike be right? I thought about my own life's journey—the challenges I faced in childhood and the stumbles I've had along the way; my string of failed relationships; and the fact that, no matter how hard I tried, I just couldn't seem to find work that fit who I was. Maybe all this imperfection in my life *was* perfect—everything had unfolded exactly as it was meant to, and there was some kind of a larger plan at play that I was missing. And perhaps all of my imperfections as a man were opportunities to grow. These thoughts made me relax and brought me an immediate sense of relief.

"Our imperfection gives meaning to our lives," Father Mike continued. "It gives us a central mission: to make the journey back to the original and ideal selves we were born as, and reclaim the people we truly are. If it weren't for our human failings, there would be no inner work for us to do on ourselves. And it's this very interior work that reconnects us to our personal magnificence. You see, Jack, to have more of what you desire in your life, you must first *become* more of who you really are. To become a success, it's not really about doing more, it's about *being* more."

"I'd agree with that for sure. I'm getting pretty tired of feeling that, no matter how much I do and no matter how many toys I gather, it's never enough."

Father Mike didn't seem to be surprised by my sentiment. "You don't like your old life, do you?"

"No, not really," I replied. "Actually, I hate it. I never seem to have any fun anymore. Everything's become so serious and

routine. God, I never thought life would be so hard, to be totally honest with you."

"Well, then, to have a new life, you must first think, feel,
and act like a new person. In life, we ultimately don't really get
what we want, we get what we *are*. To have new things in your
life, such as a new relationship, new levels of joy, and new experiences of fulfillment, you must begin to do new things."

"Such as?"

"Such as really getting to know your weaknesses. That's a
great place to start; in fact, it's where I started. Clearing up your
weaknesses is one of the primary reasons we're here. The purpose of our lives, in so many ways, is to come to terms with our
darkness so that we can live in our light. We all have our blind
spots—we need to acknowledge them and bring them into the
light of awareness, where they'll be healed. And we need to
reconfigure our false beliefs and work through our blocked emo-
tions. Ironically, in moving ahead, we're essentially going
back—back to the beautiful and perfect creatures we were at
birth."

Father Mike surveyed the cathedral and then smiled. "I used
to be one mean character," he admitted. "I really didn't care
about anyone but myself in my youth. In my relationships with
other human beings, all I'd focus on was what *I* wasn't getting.
Then one day while I was studying in France, I got a phone call
informing me that my kid brother had been killed in a nightclub
shooting. That event devastated me and changed everything. I
began to pray for guidance and the courage to get through that
period of my life. It was so rough at times that I thought about
taking my own life. But the more I prayed, the more I started to
see that my life had meaning and that I was needed in the world.
I eventually began to study theology and finally ended up here
as a priest. And now, in my relationships, I don't think about

what I'll get from someone else. Instead, all I care about is what I can give. And that, my friend, has made me a very happy man."

He paused and then yelled once again: "Welcome to Roma!"

I couldn't help but laugh at his somewhat eccentric behavior.

"Jack, let me tell you something: What you don't own about yourself owns you," Father Mike continued as we entered the main room of the cathedral.

"I wasn't aware of this."

"It's true. If you don't own that dark part of you that's selfish, for example, it will own you. If you don't own that part of you that feels that you'll never be good enough, to use another common example, it will own you. If you don't own up to a dark part of yourself that mistrusts other human beings, it will own you and in various ways run—and then ruin—your life. It wasn't until I owned my selfishness when I was younger that I began to change, you know."

"This makes sense. I wonder why I've never learned this stuff. I guess I've been so busy with the trivial things in life that I've missed out on the larger picture," I said thoughtfully.

"It's a common thing to do. Many people in the world are asleep to their lives and this wisdom, but now you're ready to get to the next step. You weren't ready for this step before, so it wasn't meant to be. But now, the time to access your greatness and to stand up for your best life has arrived. Your life wouldn't have led you here were you prepared to settle for anything less."

"I agree."

"Okay. Anyway, most people deny and avoid connecting to their disowned, shadow selves. Wise people know these parts even better than those that they present to the world. Only when you understand this essential principle will you be able to find the inner peace and outer joy that you deserve. Because it's only when you know and then accept *all* of yourself that you can truly love yourself. And without self-love, there can be no peace; and without peace there's no joy. Paradoxically, though, the more you discover your light as a human being and let it beam brightly out into the world, the more the unimpressive parts you've hidden away from yourself start to reveal themselves."

"That's so true," I responded. "I've seen that happen in my intimate relationships. For instance, I'd fall in love and open up like I never had before. I'd be more caring and passionate than ever before, but then all my ugly stuff would also start showing up. It actually happened in my last relationship. I felt more love for Jane than I ever thought I could experience. A fantastic part of me came to life with her: We'd dance for hours in her kitchen and sing under the full moon. We'd tell each other our deepest secrets well into the night, and we'd support each other's dreams in a way I'd never thought possible. But with all that love, for some reason my worst traits appeared, and it really got messy at times. I guess it was because I felt so safe with her. And when we feel safe, it seems that our true selves peek through the social armor most of us have constructed to look good to the world."

"Perfectly put, Jack. I'll add this to what you've so perceptively noticed: If you study how nature works, you'll know how life works. The laws that govern nature are the same laws that run our lives. For example, have you ever noticed that it's when the sun shines the brightest that our shadows appear the biggest?"

"Sure," I replied.

"Well that's true for us as human beings as well."

"Nice metaphor, Father Mike," I said appreciatively.

"It's so easy, when we haven't done much interior work on ourselves, to believe that we're highly evolved and operating at our best. When something negative happens, we think it's another's fault. This is because all of the limiting beliefs, false assumptions, and emotional baggage that keeps us small has been conveniently hidden within a deep, dark place within us. We don't even know it's down there, running our lives and sabotaging our dreams. We begin to believe that we're ideal in many ways. We buy our own propaganda so that we don't have to face our weaknesses and do the work involved to turn them into strengths. It takes tremendous internal strength to go into that darkness that keeps us small in our lives. It takes great inner power to take a serious look at the way we're living and make the midcourse corrections that will set us back on track."

"How so?"

"Because looking at our human failings provokes the awareness that we must change, and human beings are naturally change resistant. There's actually hardwiring in our brains that wants us to remain in our routines. Science has shown that there's an ancient part of our brains known as the *amygdala* that craves routine and resents any personal change. It seeks nothing more than constant safety and control. This tendency served our earliest ancestors and helped them survive in primitive times, but it no longer serves us in our current world."

"So how do we overcome the tendency of this part of the brain?" I asked with curiosity.

"I suggest that, on a daily basis, you set your intention to consciously make changes. I've learned in my own life that my intentions shape my reality. Look for ways to stretch yourself: Teach your brain that change is good and keep blazing a path that no one else has walked, in terms of the way you show up as a person."

At this point, Father Mike did something that startled, and then amused, me. He started running past the empty pews in the grand room we were in and ducked into a small room off to the side. The next thing I knew, Frank Sinatra's classic song "My Way" was blaring, and Father Mike was dancing happily with his eyes closed. I just watched the man, unsure of what was really going on.

After the song ended, Father Mike opened his eyes. "I used to be so scared to dance," he stated. "Now I love it! It helps me keep my heart open. What I just did was take a risk, Jack. I've been so afraid to dance in front of people, so now I make it a point to confront my fears and chase my demons."

"Interesting," was the only reply I could muster.

"I constantly look for ways to put myself into situations that challenge me to heal my greatest fears. This strategy has worked amazingly well. By the way, what do you think of my moves?" he asked with a big smile. "Am I ready for MTV?"

"Not quite," I laughed.

"All I'm really suggesting is that you dedicate yourself to constant and never-ending self-discovery. That's the only way to reclaim the fullness of your light, as far as I can tell. As Erich Fromm once stated: 'Man's main task in life is to give birth to himself, to become what he potentially is.' And when you do, the most beautiful vision of reality you could ever experience begins to unfold for you. This is for certain.

"Anyway, your dad spoke of you with great love while he was here. So I know quite a few things about you."

"Like what?"

"I know that you loved to swim as a child. I know that you had great dreams when you were younger. And I know that you love chocolate," he said as he pulled out a candy bar from his pocket. Here, take a bite," he insisted.

"It tastes bittersweet," I said as we walked through the magnificent cathedral.

"Yes, just like life. You see, Jack, life has its highs and its lows. Most of us get caught up in the drama of it all. When things are good, we feel happy. When things go bad, we feel sad. This kind of approach to living is a weak way to live. You become like a piece of driftwood floating with the tides. You shift according to the current: One minute you're moving in one direction, the next you're moving in another. A far wiser way to play the game is to let go of any judgment. Stop labeling the experiences of your life and simply accept them without resistance. The next step is to then understand that life is nothing more than a growth school, and *everything* that happens to you is beautiful."

"Everything? It seems hard to accept that the death of a loved one or the loss of a relationship that brought so much happiness is a beautiful thing."

"It's only our limited human thinking that makes a thing right or wrong," Father Mike responded. "An occurrence in our lives has no *natural* right or wrong to it—it simply is. But in our human tendency to control things, we rush to label it."

"As either good or bad," I broke in.

"Yes. But there really are no good events, nor are there any bad events when you really go deep into the thick of the way the world works. *Everything* that happens to you is simply an opportunity to grow and heal a part of you that's in need of healing. The wise see this and then seize these opportunities to flourish into more of who they truly are. And that's why I say that life is a growth school."

I wondered about this concept, still uncertain about the whole notion. Could our lives actually be designed for this purpose?

Father Mike continued. "Every day, as you go out into the world, you're really going off to school. And just as in a traditional school, there's a curriculum with different courses that offer different lessons. Once you pass a course by learning its lesson, you move on to the next course."

"And if I don't get the lesson?"

"Ah, then you repeat the course—of course," he noted seriously. "It's called *recycling*. Every experience that intersects with your life comes to you to teach you the lesson you most need to learn to rise to the next platform of your life. When the student is ready, the teacher always appears."

"Cal told me that," I said softly, feeling some sadness coming up over the loss of the father I'd only briefly known.

"That's because I told it to him first," Father Mike replied with a smile. "Anyway, if you get this process and realize the opportunity for a lesson in *every* situation, you can move on to the next course. And as you move on from the old course, you also move on from your old life because, interestingly enough, once you get the needed lesson, the type of person or situation that the lesson came wrapped up within never visits you again. It's almost as if we shed an old skin each time we get a new lesson, pass a new course, and move on to the next, higher parts of our life paths."

"A very brilliant setup, the way it all works," I reflected.

"It is. But if you *don't* accept the learning that the experience represents, let's say because you blame the other person involved for whatever transpired, and fail to see the point of wisdom that you were destined to learn, the circumstance will continue to repeat or recycle in your life until you finally get it. And the more you miss the lessons being presented, the more painful each event that carries them to you becomes until a time eventually comes when you're suffering so much that your only option is to get it."

"Remarkable—the working of the world is more extraordinary than I ever imagined," I said excitedly, feeling more comfortable with this unconventional philosophy of life I was being exposed to.

"Yes, Jack, that's true. These natural laws that govern all things never cease to amaze me. Anyway, what I'm really saying is this: *Your current reality is nothing more than a complete reflection of the lessons you most need to learn.*"

"That's a very powerful statement, Father Mike. Revolutionary, as a matter of fact."

"Yes. And since you learn far more from what's not working in your life than from what is, all that's not working is a gift. Milton Erickson wrote: 'Life will bring you pain all by itself. Your responsibility is to create joy.' Since you discover more about yourself through failure than through success, make failure a friend that you value and learn from. Create joy through it."

"What do you mean by 'make failure a friend'?"

"Well, every single thing that you hate about your life, every single thing that irritates you in your days, and every single thing that causes you stress is a very important teacher. The things that press your buttons offer your best clues about what needs to grow and evolve within you. The things that you dislike about your life—your irritations and your stressors—are all nothing more than vehicles that carry the lessons you need to learn to pass the course you're currently in and move on to the next one."

"In doing so, I'll move on to the next part of my life?"

"Exactly."

"So all the things I don't like about my life are actually my best friends and greatest teachers because they help me get to my destination—my ideal life," I summarized.

"And your highest self. I'll talk more about all this later, but for now, just know that life is this extraordinary growth school and everything that happens to you is quite divine. It *is* a very amazing setup, really, the way this intelligent universe of ours works," Father Mike observed.

He paused and looked deeply into my eyes. "Any questions?"

"Well, I'd love some examples of recycling. I think this would help me spot the process when it occurs in my life."

"Sure. If the lesson you most need to learn at a certain stage of your life is acceptance, you might notice that a constant stream of people who drive you crazy are entering your life. Or, if your lesson is to be less controlling, you might notice many controlling people surfacing in your day. Reminds me of what Buddha said so many years ago: 'Imagine that every person in the world is enlightened but you. They are all your teachers, each doing just the right things to help you learn patience, perfect wisdom, perfect compassion.'"

"Great words—but I'm surprised that a priest would be quoting Buddha," I said.

"Well, Jack, ultimately my quest is the quest for truth. And all of the great religions of the world speak of the same truth. So if Buddha arrived at a point of wisdom that's worthy of my sharing, I feel compelled to share it with you."

"Good answer," I said playfully, clapping my hands and mimicking a game-show host.

"So back to the process of recycling," Father Mike said as he began to arrange a stunning bouquet of flowers that had been placed on a small table at the front of the room we were in. "If you don't have the awareness to know that this is what's happening and deny personal responsibility for your role in the scenarios you're drawing into your life, then these types of people—or should I say teachers—will keep appearing in your life. They'll continue to recycle, and in progressively more painful ways, until you see *your* role and *your* opportunity for advancement in each interaction."

"So it's not until *I* take some real responsibility in every instance of my life that I can grow and my life can improve. Is that the real message?"

"Right. And then—and this is the amazing part—those kinds of people and situations will stop showing up in your life."

"Incredible. Absolutely incredible."

"Well, it's actually not as black-and-white as that, I must admit. Once you get the lesson, a few things could happen. These kinds of people may just stop appearing with the frequency they used to because they came to you as teachers and now their work has been done."

"Okay. What's another possibility?"

"The behavior of these people might change dramatically, and all of a sudden, they'll appear to be the kindest, most loving souls you've ever met."

"How could they change so immediately?"

"One explanation is that, in shifting from blaming them, as most of us tend to do in such situations, to working on yourself and clearing up the blocks that need to be cleared within you, you powerfully create a space *for them* to become their best selves in the situations that previously caused them to be difficult. People are essentially good, you know. And if you shower them with unconditional love and understanding rather than attack and blame, they cannot help but respond in higher and more enlightened ways than they've historically acted. In the face of true love and deep caring, no human being can stay out of their hearts. All shadows die in the light. Another explanation is this one: We do a dance with each and every person who's important to us in our lives."

"Oh, not more dancing," I said with a quick laugh.

"This is different. This is the dance of relationship and, again, we all do it. You could actually draw a flowchart of the dance you do with each of the significant people in your life if you wanted to get really clear on it. Let's say, for example, that the woman you're dating tells you to clean up the dishes after you've had dinner. This might be the triggering event that sets the dance into motion. Your reaction might be to feel controlled by her and get irritated. She then gets her buttons pushed, so her step in the dance might be to feel guilty and small for hurting your feelings, which she manifests as anger. And so it goes—the two of you do an elaborate dance of one reactionary step after another that you're not even aware of. Each of you pushes the other's buttons, which are nothing more than old hurts from the past that have never been resolved and healed. Actually, most of these wounds are from childhood and have nothing to do with the person you're with now.

"In many relationships, the same dance repeats itself for decades. And because both partners are unconscious of it, and have no commitment to doing the inner work required to become aware of the pattern at play, it continues. Now here's the point I'm getting to: You can change the entire dynamic of any relationship the moment you stop dancing. As soon as you recognize that the dance has started, just stop doing the move you always do—just opt out of the whole pattern and take the higher road."

"How would I do that?" I asked.

"Well, in the scenario I've given you, just before you go into your regular reaction of getting irritated when you feel controlled, catch your thinking and choose a higher alternative. Each time you're just about to go into your old, self-defeating behavior, make a wiser choice. When you do this, the energy that the old behavior had over you will be transmuted into positive personal power. And each time you do this, you'll actually create new pathways in your brain, which will then make way for new behaviors to express themselves in your life. This is the best way to grow more powerful as a human being—just keep choosing the highest, *most loving* possible response in every situation. It'll get easier in time, and the results will be astounding.

"So in the scenario we're discussing, let's say that instead of getting irritated with your date, you dig deep into yourself and realize that she's really not trying to control you at all. You realize that you're simply projecting the controlling behavior your mother used to visit on you onto your date. In other words, this irritation you feel is not about your current partner at all, but about something you've never resolved around your mother. Your date asking you to clean up the dishes was simply the triggering event that sent you back to childhood. You realize this, and in doing so, you've just stopped dancing. And when you stop dancing with someone, what does that force them to do?"

"Well, they can't keep dancing alone, can they?" I guessed.

"Exactly. So by changing *your* behavior, they must necessarily change *their* behavior. That's why it's so much more powerful to work on changing yourself rather than wasting your energies in trying to change the other person. And that's why seeing the opportunity for growth in every single situation of your life and then taking personal responsibility rather than blaming someone else is actually the best way to influence the other person to change."

"What you've just shared with me will transform my relationships!" I exclaimed.

"And of course there will be situations where your partner *has* done something wrong," Father Mike continued. "In these situations, just remember that the antidote to fear is love. When you step back from a challenging situation and see that a person who's acting harshly is really crying out to you for help because they're either frightened or hurt at their core, then you can easily give them love. Never forget that immediately prior to any person reacting with anger or in a less-than-loving way, they experienced hurt. That's a big point. People who lash out angrily have done so because they've just been hurt. They need your caring—not your condemnation. Remember, when you give them the love that every human being craves, their best selves will peek through because you've created a safe space for them to shine. When you change, others automatically change because you've given them room to bloom."

— ✦ —

What Father Mike had been telling me was extremely potent. And it made complete sense. The more I reflected on his theory about the way the world operates, the more I saw how the process of recycling had been playing out my entire life without my awareness. I went through the same kinds of experiences and people over and over. For example, I kept attracting sales clients at work who would promise big deals but they'd never come through, causing me endless disappointment and costing the agency a ton of cash. I also seemed to run across more than my fair share of people I felt were rude to me—often everyone I interacted with in a single day seemed to have a chip on their shoulder and a negative attitude. If what Father Mike was saying was true, these were not random events. Rather, they were part of a script that had been written for me, part of a growth school I'd been attending since birth. And the only reason these people kept coming and these events kept repeating was because *I* wasn't getting the life lesson that I was required to learn.

I began to think even more deeply about the people that filled my life. For some reason, I kept on attracting girlfriends who wanted a deeper relationship than I was ready for. The more they expressed their need for this, the more aloof I became, fearing the loss of personal freedom I perceived a truly intimate relationship would cause. Maybe, just maybe, this kept on occurring for a reason—there was a lesson for me to learn in this scenario that kept on recycling itself throughout my life.

What could the lesson be? Perhaps it was time for me to open my heart and let another human being in, evolving into a kinder, more loving person in the process. Was I replaying a pattern I'd picked up unconsciously from my parents' relationship? Well, maybe it was time for me to stop being so afraid of losing my freedom and discover that the true joy in life appears once it's shared with someone you love.

I'd never done this kind of self-reflection before. I'd never made the time in my life to go deep and look at my negative traits and behaviors. It was kind of like doing detective work, bringing awareness to the lost parts of myself. But now, I could see that it was one of the most important activities that a person could perform. A person who doesn't truly know themselves really knows nothing. And perhaps the reason for my tragic accident was to cause me to go within.

When life is smooth and steady, I've come to realize, we tend to live it on a superficial level. When life gets tough and we experience a crisis, we always end up doing some internal reflection and introspection. And so I think that the mystics and sages of the past were right when they observed that life's greatest difficulties are actually life's biggest blessings, for they serve to deepen us and open us up to a wider experience of living. Breakdowns always lead to breakthroughs.

The more I thought, the more I saw the patterns that kept recurring in my life. I seemed to draw an inordinate number of people into my life who expressed things in a way that often hurt my feelings. Maybe this was all unfolding in this way because I was to learn a life lesson here. Perhaps, as I reflected, my self-worth needed to improve and I had to take things less personally.

Suddenly, the skeptical side of me spoke up, wondering if life really did work this way. Maybe Father Mike, well intentioned as he was, was a dreamer, great at voicing intriguing theories but detached from the real world. Then that word flashed across my consciousness again: *trust*. In my gut, I knew that he spoke the truth. And that was all I really needed to know.

"Okay, my young friend," Father Mike said, breaking my reverie. He took my knapsack from me and led me up a circular staircase. "Enough for one day. Let me show you to your room—I know you'll love the view. It looks out over the whole city of Rome. At night, you can watch the shooting stars. This will be your home for the next month. Oh, before I forget, let me give you the key."

Father Mike handed me a golden key attached to a metal tag and then walked me into the guest room. It was small and sparsely furnished but meticulously clean. A single gerbera—the flower of happiness—rested in a silver vase on the nightstand. And the view was, as promised, spectacular. As I turned to thank Father Mike for his generosity of spirit, I realized he'd left. Then I looked at the tag attached to the key. It had a quote inscribed on it. Here's what it said:

*"The only devils in the world are those running in our own hearts.
That is where the battle should be fought."*

— Mahatma Gandhi

4 TO THINE OWN SELF BE TRUE

"We can easily forgive a child who is afraid of the dark.
The real tragedy of life is when an adult is afraid of the light."

— Plato

"Behind all seen things lies something vaster; everything is
but a path, a portal, or a window opening on something
other than itself."

— Antoine de Saint-Exupéry

——— ✦ ———

I slept more deeply than I had in a long time and dreamed a wonderful dream—that I was a child again, full of joy, passion, and innocence. I was dancing barefoot in a small mountain meadow, surrounded by snowcapped peaks and flower-filled valleys. I could hear other children laughing and playing as I danced, caught up in the wonder of the moment. My heart felt happy, my mind was quiet, and I was completely at peace.

I was awakened by a gentle hand. It was Father Mike nudging me to wake up. He was smiling, and his eyes twinkled as he expressed his gratitude for the beautiful morning that had unfolded outside.

"It's another great day out there, Jack," he said. "Let's not miss a moment of it. I have so much to share with you. Why don't you get ready and meet me downstairs? We can have a quick breakfast and then go sit on the front steps."

"Perfect," I replied. "I have a few questions that I'd love to ask you that have come up since our conversation yesterday."

"Perfect," Father Mike echoed.

It truly was a magnificent morning, and the steps of the cathedral were a great place to sit. The smell of the roses that rested alongside us was enchanting, and watching all the people walk by on the street deepened my connection to the ancient city of Rome, where so much of the world's wisdom had been created.

"Yesterday you told me that life is a growth school, Father Mike. Every person and every experience comes to us to teach us the lesson we most need to learn at that particular point of our journey. We can either awaken to this act of nature, or we can turn a blind eye to it and, in doing so, keep repeating the mistakes of the past until the pain becomes so great that we have no choice but to change."

"Nice summary," Father Mike said as he munched on a freshly baked piece of bread topped with Gorgonzola cheese. "Soon the student will become the teacher," he added encouragingly.

"Well, I'm wondering, does everyone have to follow the same curriculum you've spoken of? I mean, do each of us have to learn the same lessons and take the same courses in this growth school?"

"Very good question, Jack. You'll do well here with me—that's for sure," Father Mike said as we relaxed in the sunlight. It was one of those days where, even though the sun was blazing, one could still see the moon in the blue sky.

"In answer to your question, each and every person on the planet has a different curriculum assigned to them—it's customized learning, if you will. The lessons I need to learn in my life, for example, are probably very different from those that are destined for you. My curriculum might be designed around teaching me to be less critical and more accepting. And my life lessons might be about becoming more giving, releasing any thoughts of scarcity, letting go of any need for control, and surrendering to the flow of life.

"On the other hand," Father Mike continued, "your curriculum might be designed to teach you to get out of your head and live more in your heart—to live in the moment and *feel* rather than to think all the time. It might be about letting go of any self-centeredness and considerations around competition—dedicating yourself to supporting others selflessly. Your learning path might be about seeing the good in everyone rather than focusing on their weaknesses. It might even be about knowing your personal value and not letting anyone ever make you feel inferior."

How perceptive, I thought. It was as if this man knew my deepest issues and my most personal inner struggles. The way he operated was masterful. My mother had a similar gift—so much of the way she lived was run from her intuition. She just *knew* the right thing to do in any given situation and trusted this knowing with all her heart. I'd always made my choices in life based on reason and logic, while I suddenly saw that Mom had come from a deeper, wiser place.

"In any event," Father Mike continued with a mouthful of bread, "all I was really trying to convey yesterday was that each event and every person that enters our lives does so for a reason.

Remember, *there are no coincidences*. The world is a giant radar, detecting our growth needs and then sending us the corresponding people and events for the promotion of this growth. A point of wisdom related to this is that the people in our lives are mirrors, reflecting the brightest as well as the darkest parts of ourselves."

"Are you serious?" I asked.

"Yes. You wouldn't be able to see the great quality of another person unless you knew that quality in yourself."

"I guess that makes sense. I wouldn't be able to recognize something good in someone else if I had no idea what it was."

"Correct. If you've never seen what caviar looks like, you wouldn't be able to recognize it on someone's plate at a fancy dinner party. Similarly, if you haven't recognized and owned a talent or positive trait within yourself, it's impossible for you to see it in another. If you don't know what it's like to truly love someone, for example, you'd have no way of knowing when someone showers you with love. If you haven't owned a personal gift—a strong intellect, for example—you won't be able to appreciate it in someone else. To see something great about another person is to see that greatness within yourself. I should mention that this principle also holds true for the negative qualities you can't stand in others."

"What do you mean?"

"Well," Father Mike replied, "for you to see another person as angry, you must first have to know what real anger looks like. For you to call someone angry, you must have anger within you. For you to perceive someone as selfish, you'd have to have some selfishness in you. For you to call someone manipulative, you'd have to have a manipulative side, too. Otherwise, there would be no way in the world you could recognize these qualities. All of life is nothing more than a projection. Like a huge movie projector, we project into our outer worlds who we are in our inner worlds. *We collect what we project.*"

"Fascinating," I responded. "Could you give me a quick example?"

"Of course. Let's say you're in a record shop. You're at one of those stations that allows you to listen to the latest recordings, and you're enjoying the tunes you're hearing. All of a sudden, one of the store clerks walks up to you and asks you to stop listening to so many at a time. He makes this request loudly and rudely. If you respond by yelling at him, to me it means that there's something within *you* that needs to be looked at and healed."

"But he was rude to *me!*" I exclaimed. "I didn't start it."

"Jack, you can't get something from nothing. All that can come out of you is what's within you—after all, you can't get tomato juice from a lemon. The very fact that this man drew anger from you by pressing your buttons means you must have had some preexisting anger within you, right?"

"I have to admit that makes sense."

"So this man triggered a part of you that's angry. If you don't own that fact, it really will keep owning you. That old anger was there before he even entered your life—it was what I call *a preexisting condition.* You need to see that and take responsibility for that rather than blaming him. He was just a catalyst. It's like what the French philosopher Antoine de Saint-Exupéry once wrote: 'No single event can awaken within us a stranger totally unknown to us. To live is to be slowly born.' So the enlightened way to look at this event in the music store is to see this rude sales clerk as a great gift. There's a huge opportunity to grow and evolve from this situation if you're wise to it. He has, by his rude behavior, introduced you to a part of yourself that's been hidden from your conscious awareness."

Father Mike took a breath and then continued. "Carl Jung once wrote that 'everything that irritates us about others can lead us to an understanding of ourselves.' Now, have the courage and maturity to do the inner work required to release your preexisting anger and shift into a space of love. That's the goal we all need to aim for—to be nothing but pure love. Because a person who's nothing but love incarnate can only see pure love when they look at another person. I know this isn't a process that can be done quickly—in many ways, it's an ideal to strive for, and for many, moving out of anger and fear into complete love and acceptance can take a lifetime of inner work. Actually, this is what the journey of life is all about—spotting our weaker areas and healing them so that we eventually find our best selves. This is the only path to walk if your objective is to find lasting peace and freedom. There's no other option."

Suddenly, Father Mike stood up and said, "C'mon. Today's a fun day. All learning and no play is no way to do things. I've discovered that self-discovery and personal growth are best accomplished in a spirit of fun and adventure—life's too short to be overly serious. Today we'll play tourists. I want to take you to the Colosseum and some of the other famous sights of Rome. And for lunch, we'll have a picnic. I even brought a little Italian wine for you," he said with a wink.

With that, this miraculous man of the cloth ran down the steps of the cathedral, smelling the roses as he descended. I couldn't wait to follow him. I knew that all his teachings were leading me home.

As the days passed, I grew more and more fond of Father Mike. He was a brilliant man, offering me insights on life that I'd never heard before, and coaching me on how I could lift my life to its highest level. But even more important, he was kind. He understood human nature, and I felt he understood me. He knew that personal change brings up our oldest and deepest demons. As we grow more into our light, our dark sides really do surface and a part of us fights to stay small, clinging to our old ways of thinking, feeling, and acting. As we get closest to love, our greatest fears come alive. Father Mike gently supported me as I embraced his philosophy and walked toward my best life. He reminded me of my magnificence and the power that each and every one of us has to shape our destinies in the moments of our days. My time with him was heaven-sent.

One morning, as we ate breakfast out on a veranda located in one wing of the cathedral, Father Mike said something that surprised me. It was during the second week I was with him, and I was feeling very happy with all the improvements I was making as a result of the ideas and tools he'd shared with me. A deep inner peace had grown within me, and I'd begun to look at all of my less-than-ideal traits and accept them for what they were: a dark side of me that needed to be healed so my light could shine. I felt happier and healthier than I'd ever felt and began to believe that this world of ours really did unfold according to a larger plan, one that had my best interests in mind. I was becoming a solid student in the growth school of life and shedding my old ways like a caterpillar sheds its cocoon once it becomes a butterfly.

"You know, Father Mike," I stated cheerfully as I bit into a fresh croissant, "this self-improvement stuff really works. I've always thought it was a waste of time. But I must admit—I'm really feeling some amazing changes within me."

"The term *self-improvement* is nonsense to me," Father Mike replied as he stared out over the still sleeping city. "It suggests that people are broken and need to be fixed. But nothing could be further from the truth. Nothing! Each one of us is perfect at our core—we just need to work through the layers to get back to our perfection."

"I thought that as a priest and my life coach, you'd be all about encouraging me to improve myself, live more nobly, and exist more wisely—to be a better, kinder, and more loving human being. What could possibly be wrong with the notion of self-improvement?" I asked, playing devil's advocate.

"It's wrong—that's what's wrong with it," he responded with even greater conviction, his voice rising passionately. "The journey of life is not about *improving* oneself, Jack. Rather—and this point is extremely important—it's about *remembering* oneself. Those of us who seek to find our best life and manifest the desires of our heart must walk the path of inner discovery, not outer change. The real goal in life is self-revelation: revealing your best self to your current self and then seeing the world through a new set of eyes in the process."

"But if no one needs to improve, why is the world in such poor shape? Why is there such evil in the world? Why are there wars and homeless people and starving children? Why is there so much hatred and so little love?"

"Slow down, Jack. All I'm saying is that no one needs to improve upon what they already are. That kind of thinking just makes people feel more guilty than they already do. For example, you, my young friend, are already perfect."

"Really?"

"Yes."

"Then why am I here as your pupil?"

"For self-discovery—not self-improvement," he stated emphatically. "That's why we're all here on the planet. It's a subtle distinction, but an essential one. I'm not going to tell you to change or improve or start acting like someone else. I'd never do that to you. My whole focus over our time together is to help you reveal your true self to yourself—to get to know yourself for the first time. This path you're traveling isn't a journey to some distant land. Rather, it leads back to a place you once knew but forgot along the way, as those around you socialized you out of your essence. Actually, it's a journey back home, to the natural greatness and perfection that you had when you were born. T. S. Eliot made the point so well when he wrote: 'We must not cease from exploration. And the end of all our exploring will be to arrive where we began and to know the place for the first time.'"

"Meaningful words."

"And accurate ones," Father Mike noted. "Life really is nothing more than a journey back home. You know, Jack, in so many ways, greatness as a human being is about nothing more than the recovery of the gifts you lost as you grew up. Living your best life is really mostly about recapturing what you gave up."

"Neat way of looking at it," I offered.

"It's true. As a child, you were aware of all your gifts. You were innocent and pure. You were immensely creative and wildly passionate. Your imagination knew no boundaries and your dreams knew no limits. You trusted others and had faith in yourself. You didn't have this need we adults have: to have everything all figured out. You expressed your truest essence as a person without fear of reprisal, and you freely let your light shine. You lived totally in the moment and savored every simple gift that each of our lives brings to us on a regular basis. You loved snowflakes and spiders, singing and dreaming, a good hug and a steaming cup of hot chocolate. The world was abundant, a place of boundless possibilities, and a ready partner for your authentic success. But then something happened."

"What?" I ask pointedly.

"Well, to put it bluntly, you committed a crime. Actually you committed the most serious crime any human being could commit."

I felt uncomfortable. Father Mike looked at me with intense seriousness, and said, "You began to betray yourself. You disowned your true self in favor of buying into the beliefs of your tribe."

"My tribe?"

"Yes, Jack. Society is your tribe. You see, you started to adopt other people's beliefs about the way the world works and the nature of your role within it. You shut down your beautiful feelings and began to live in your mind—spending your days rationalizing, judging, and worrying rather than skipping, dancing, and playing. You became a pleaser—thinking, acting, and conducting yourself in ways that were not of your own choosing but of the choosing of those around you, such as your parents, teachers, and friends. And so the process of socialization took over and your personal magnificence began to be hidden. You did what you were told, acted as you were instructed to act, and thought the way people taught you to think."

"And in doing so, I began to live in a small box, so to speak," I added.

"Precisely. After you die, there will be plenty of time to be in a small box . . . so why live in one while you're alive?"

"Good point," I responded, getting the graphic picture my very wise teacher had painted. "But surely you're not saying that it's wrong for parents to teach their kids manners and to be responsible in the world. Or do you have a problem with teachers showing discipline and adults setting limits?"

"Yes and no. Of course it's important for parents to be leaders and wise guides for their children. Without discipline and healthy boundaries, a child would be lost. But life is all about balance—and that's one of the most important principles I can teach you. Sure, a child needs to be schooled on what good behavior looks like, and no doubt a child needs to be taught about limits. Certain limits placed on a child's behavior are essential, but any limits placed on a child's *spirit* are not."

"I get your point."

"May I borrow your childhood experience for a moment?'

"Sure, Father Mike," I said as I sat up in my chair.

"I'll bet that, after the age of three or four, most of the way you conducted yourself was done simply to make your mother or your father or your teachers proud of you. Every child needs love and craves approval, so you began to betray yourself and act in inauthentic ways for the sake of making the people you loved as happy as you could. You believed that the best way to secure their love was to act as they wanted you to act. Rather than singing at the top of your lungs at the supermarket and letting your genuine self be revealed to the world, you sang softly so that your mother wouldn't feel embarrassed and get annoyed with you."

"And I've been singing softly ever since, figuratively speaking," I responded, gaining a deep appreciation of the wisdom I was hearing.

"Right. What did Thoreau once say? 'Most people die with their music still within them.'"

"He also said, 'If a man does not keep pace with his companions, perhaps it is because he hears a different drummer. Let him step to the music which he hears, however measured and far away,'" I added, remembering the words of this great American philosopher whose life I had studied in school.

"Lovely," said Father Mike with his eyes closed, soaking up the knowledge conveyed in the rich words I'd shared. "All of us need to give all of the people around us permission to be their true selves. We must, as you suggest, let people march to their own beat and feel safe to be real around us. That's what *unconditional* love is all about—being an encourager of people's passions, loves, and dreams—even if you don't agree with them. And those powerful words you just shared, in turn, make me think of an ancient Sanskrit verse that says: 'Spring has past, summer has gone, and spring is here. And the song that I meant to sing remains unsung.' Most people do die with the great song of their lives remaining unsung. They fail to live the gorgeous lives that they were meant to. And this isn't only a great disservice to ourselves—it's a great disservice to the world."

Father Mike sipped his cappuccino for a moment, and then resumed speaking. "When we live our best lives, our true lives, our authentic lives, we become *all* of our brilliance. And when we show up in the world this way, the world benefits by the things that we do. It's like what Paolo Coelho, author of the incredible book *The Alchemist* wrote: 'The world will be either better or worse depending on whether we become better or worse.'"

"My God! That's a great way to look at it," I said passionately.

Father Mike went on. "Unfortunately, most people never get this. They never realize that their lives mean too much to the world—they must have the bravery to become who they truly are. And so, Jack, their once-beautiful lives become a charade. Far too many of us don't live in a way that's true to ourselves. We live our mother's life, our father's life, or even our priest's life, rather than having the courage to live the lives that were uniquely meant for us. To me, that is the ultimate sin."

"I hear you, Father," I said respectfully.

He continued his discourse. "Rather than dreaming of becoming an astronaut or a poet or a statesman, I'd be willing to bet that as you aged you resigned yourself to becoming something that your teacher told you was more practical to become. Rather than being authentic and saying what you really meant to say in any given situation, you began to wear a social mask and think, feel, and act according to what others told you was the proper way to think, feel, and act. You began to deny yourself, to yourself. You became 'A Great Pretender.' Essentially, you stifled your self-expression and lost your voice."

"So true," I admitted.

"In not expressing yourself and your truth, you lost the voice that expresses the real you to the world. And a person without self-expression is a person without personal freedom. A person who doesn't genuinely show who they are to the world also becomes invisible, mere figments of their real selves."

"I committed self-betrayal," I agreed, declaring my understanding the concept.

Father Mike nodded. "And the more you lost sight of your natural magnificence and who you truly are, the more you grew into being someone you weren't. And the more you acted that way, the more you lost respect for yourself. Your self-worth began to diminish in deep ways. And day by day, the deepest part of you began to shut down and disconnect with the true you. We forget that a great life is an authentic life. As the poet David Whyte has said, 'The soul would rather fail at its own life than succeed at someone else's.' And yet we forget this truth. That kills a person, Jack. A part of them begins to die."

"Then why do we do it? And why don't we remedy the problem?" I asked.

"Because of fear. First we fear being different. We want to fit into the tribe and be a part of the community. There's a huge value placed in our world on doing what everyone else is doing and thinking as everyone else is thinking. *What will my friends think if I walk my own path and don't buy into their ways?* we wonder. *What will the neighbors think if little Johnny wants to become a poet instead of a doctor?* our parents ask themselves. And in thinking this way, as parents ourselves, we play God with our children's lives, which is a sad thing to do to any human being. Rather than trusting in them and creating a safe environment to allow their best selves to grow, we tell children what they should do when they grow up so we can impress the people next door. The truth of the matter is that parents do this because of *their* own fears. Parents tell their kids that they must be doctors or lawyers or marry into the right families because of their own fears of looking like failures if their children don't become 'successful' by the definition of success in our society.

"But what is success anyway? To me, *success is nothing more than living your life according to your own truth and on your own terms.* It's adhering to the values that speak to the best within you, regardless of the external pressures of society. Success is living your life in the process of creating and realizing what's most important to you—not what's most important to anyone else. That's how the spiritual heavyweights who've walked the planet before you have lived. And that's my recommendation to you. Trust me on this. This point of wisdom alone, if integrated into each and every one of the days that you have left, will cause you to live an extraordinary life."

Father Mike paused, looked up to the sky for a moment as if

to seek guidance from the heavens, and then continued. "The second reason we betray ourselves and borrow someone else's life path is because we fear our own light."

"What do you mean by that?"

"Jack, every single person on this planet has more power slumbering within us than we could ever imagine. If we only knew how powerful and magnificent we were, we really would worship ourselves daily. We'd go to the altar of our lives and honor ourselves constantly. We'd love ourselves completely and would be the hero and idol of our lives. We wouldn't have the fears we have, and we wouldn't limit ourselves in the way we do. But sadly, the power we have within us also scares us. With great talent also comes great responsibility. At a deep level within ourselves, we wonder whether we can handle the dazzling potential that exists within us, and we're afraid of the guilt that we'll feel if we mishandle or squander our natural power."

"So we deny it," I observed. "And in doing so, my guess would be that we also deny our destinies as well."

"Very good, young Jack. Very good," remarked Father Mike, clearly impressed with my participation in the conversation. "We go into what psychologists call *denial*. This is a coping mechanism every human being employs to avoid feeling the pain of the truth. What we all do is create a story or use even stronger language—we lie about something and then we fool our conscious minds into believing it's true, even though our souls know it's a lie."

"Wow."

"Denial operates at a level below the conscious mind, so we don't even know we're doing it. Yes, as you say, we deny our light. But just as tragic is the fact we deny our darkness as well. Each and every one of us has this hidden part of us, this shadow self I've been alluding to over these past days—a segment of ourselves that we don't want to acknowledge, for doing so would make us feel ashamed. This is the part of us that feel jealous when others succeed; that seeks to hoard when another is in need; that acts critical when we should offer love; that acts in a controlling way when we should be acting in a supporting way; and that feels competition when we should see that all of us are connected and when one of us wins, we all win. Every single person on the planet has a portion of ourselves that we hide from the world. In our endless quest to appear perfect, we put it away in a dark box. We actually deny its very existence and in doing so, we deny a part of ourselves."

"I've been thinking a lot about this concept since I've been with you," I said.

"Great, Jack. But there's more. Because we deny a part of ourselves, we can never be fully alive. Showing leadership in your life involves having the inner strength to accept *every* part of yourself, the parts that please you and the parts that don't. Once you do, you'll develop an appreciation of self that will connect you to your best life quite quickly. You'll become whole again— and to become whole is to become healthy. But so few people do this. It's so much easier to deny our imperfect parts, to present ourselves to the world as flawless and wear the mask of perfection. And even though deep down we know it's a lie, we do it anyway."

"So this concept of denial you've mentioned keeps us trapped in a lie, in a sense."

"That's exactly what it does. That's precisely what denial is all about—lying to yourself to avoid the pain of owning up to the truth. At a deep level, you just may be out of integrity. Sure, you know how to talk like someone who has high integrity, and you tell yourself that you're a good person who has high moral standards. But if you really get truthful with yourself, you might start to see your denial. You might start to notice all the times you tell little lies or cut ethical corners. You convince yourself that you're impeccably honest—but are you? And you think no one notices, but someone does see every thought, act, and feeling. And that someone is *you*.

"Every one of us has a soul within us that knows what it means to be a decent, loving, and noble human being. We all have a deep place inside of us that *knows*. When you do something wrong, you can try to fool yourself by rationalizing what you did at a conscious level. You can create a whole story about how the world is out of integrity and you're the victim. You can build a case that the other person deserved what they did to you and you acted harshly with them to teach them a lesson. But it's not your responsibility to serve as policeman of the universe. Your job is to show up as a leader within your own life by getting the lessons that this growth school is delivering to you, and by doing so, evolve into your authentic and best self."

"Okay," I said, trying to take this all in, "would it be fair to say that this war is one of authenticity? Or more accurately, it's a battle for integrity—since when we act in ways that aren't congruent with who we truly are, we're out of integrity?"

"Most definitely, Jack. There's an extremely powerful concept I call The Integrity Gap. Simply stated, the greater the gap between who you are on the inside, or your true self, and the way you occur on the outside, or your social self, the greater the unhappiness you'll feel in your life. As Ashley Montague noted so many years ago: 'The deepest personal defeat suffered by human beings is constituted by the difference between what one was capable of becoming and what one has in fact become.' You see, the main reason so many millions of people in our world today have this spiritual malaise that they carry around with them every waking moment is because of The Integrity Gap. They're betraying themselves and not letting their true essence shine in the world. And the deepest and best parts of them certainly know it."

"My mother used to tell me, 'Jack, who you are as a person speaks so loudly that I can't hear what you're saying,'" I said.

"Wise woman. And she was right—we all must let our lives speak for themselves. Who you are as a person and the way you show up in life says it all. And you need to be true to yourself, otherwise it all catches up with you.

"It's so beautifully set up," Father Mike said, and then he chuckled.

"Why are you laughing?"

"Because the world operates with such extraordinary intelligence and the design of the universe is so perfect that I can only laugh at how we, as human beings, think we're in control of it all! I mean, look at the way this is all orchestrated. Just think about it for a minute," he said, his eyes boring into mine. "You have all this potential slumbering inside of you. You have certain values you hold dearest to you. You have certain ways of thinking, feeling, and acting that are part of what make you unique on this planet. You have certain passions and preferences that make you happy. And certain dreams for your life that are encoded in you as deeply as your DNA. All these things are aspects of your true self. And as you move away from living a life that reflects these aspects of your true self—by not shining in the world, doing the things you love, living according to your most important values, feeling your feelings, or speaking your truth—you slowly close down. Your self-worth plummets, and your soul begins to wrinkle. The amount of unhappiness you experience increases. You have less energy, your creativity diminishes, and you have no passion."

"So the malaise I feel is a gift," I said, deducing a big insight.

"You *are* smart," Father Mike said as he clapped his hands proudly. "That's it! All the dissatisfaction you feel is really nothing more than your best life—your destiny knocking at the door of your current life. The ache you feel in your inner core is your spirit telling you to wake up and get back on track—to become congruent and authentic and be the person that you truly are. As Hermann Hesse wrote in *Demian:* 'Each man has only one genuine vocation—to find the way to himself. . . . His task was to discover his own destiny—not an arbitrary one—and live it out wholly and resolutely within himself. Everything else was only a would-be existence, an attempt at evasion, a flight back to the ideals of the masses, conformity and fear of one's own inwardness.' The sad thing is that most people pay no attention to this malaise, this emptiness, this inner longing that exits within them, this universal prompting to awaken and discover their best selves. They believe that their unhappiness is natural."

"So how do I align my outer world with my inner world?" I wondered.

"You should consciously begin to take steps every day to close the integrity gap, Jack. By doing so, you'll reclaim the person that you truly are. And when that happens, greatness infuses every dimension of your life."

"Where do I start?"

"First, you need to go deep inside and begin the process of knowing yourself. Self-knowledge is the starting point of personal excellence. Detect your largest values, define how you really wish to conduct your life, and think about what makes you happy. Clarify what standards you feel you need to live your life under in order to be true to yourself, then articulate how you'd occur in the world if you were really thinking, acting, and feeling in authentic ways. What would it all look like? What things would you no longer tolerate? What activities would you no longer participate in, and which people would you consciously choose to remove from your life?"

"Interesting questions," I remarked.

"I suggest that you actually write down what you discover in that journal I gave you on your first day here so that you can form an ongoing dialogue with yourself. It's very important to have conversations with yourself so that you'll get to know who you really are. Then the next step is to take action each day to reveal the true you to the world—to close The Integrity Gap. Start to live your life on your own terms."

"Close the gap," I echoed.

"Yes—be authentic, be real, and be yourself. And the moment you do, your self-esteem will grow by leaps and bounds, and you'll unleash a remarkable degree of confidence. You won't even know what's happening, as this all will take place at a very deep subconscious level. But you'll start to see big changes in the way you operate when your *social* self becomes a mirror reflection of your *true* self. You'll have incredible amounts of energy and will find that you're more creative than ever. You'll notice that you have a deep sense of joy and peace within you. Being true to yourself lifts your life to a whole new level and awakens your best self. From a metaphysical viewpoint, when you align your outer world with your inner world, the universe throws its winds beneath your wings and send you more of its treasures."

Father Mike stood up. "Meet me in the Grand Room tomorrow morning at seven. I need to show you something," he said with a hint of mystery. "That's it for today. I've given you a lot to think about, so I suggest that you retire to your room and do some journaling. Record what you've learned from me and what you've discovered about yourself. I know this practice will be most helpful to you."

And with that, he was off, leaving me with a mind full of thoughts and a sense of hope that I hadn't known for many years.

5 THE STAINED GLASS WINDOW

"The level of thinking that got you to where you now are
will not get you to where you dream of being."

— Albert Einstein

"There is a giant asleep within everyone.
When that giant awakens, miracles happen."

— Frederick Faust

"Come with me. I want to show you something," said Father Mike when he and I met the next morning.

I followed him as he walked to the center of the largest room in the cathedral. He pointed to the remarkable stained glass window that was the stunning highlight of the entire space. The sun radiated through its different colored pieces, creating a rainbow that filled the room with spectacular light.

"Each and every one of us sees the world through our own personal stained glass window, Jack. Your life can change once you really understand this point. Mine did."

"Really?"

"Yes. We see the world not as it is but as *we* are," Father Mike observed. "Each one of us walks out into the world every day and thinks that the way we experience the world before us is the experience of truth. But that's more of our arrogance peeping through and our denial at play. The truth in any situation is colored by our internal stained glass window, which acts as our filter on the world. And just as that glass up there takes the light striking it and colors it, every belief, fear, assumption, and bias we carry with us colors our experience of the moment. We think we all see life through the same set of eyes as everybody else, but we don't. That's just a big lie that we fool ourselves into believing. Each one of us views the world through the lens of our personal context, which has been shaped by the unique experiences of our lives. And since no one on the planet has had exactly the same experiences, no one on the planet has the same personal experience of any given situation. Your life takes on a whole new sense of meaning the moment you truly get this. This is a very important point of wisdom I'm offering to you, Jack."

"Fascinating knowledge. I guess I've never stepped out of my own thinking and wondered whether it accurately reflected the truth or not," I admitted.

"Each one of us sees the world through our own unique set of filters, which represents our mental model. This 'stained glass window of the mind' colors how we see the world and what we believe about ourselves. Leadership of our lives requires us to realize that the way we see the world isn't necessarily a true reflection of the facts. We're not always seeing things unfolding the way we think we are."

"That's a very scary thought, Father," I stated. "It kind of makes me feel uncomfortable to believe that it's true. It makes me worry."

"That's good, Jack. You're feeling fear again, which is a nat-ural human reaction that's certain to come up when we're stretched to think or do something new in our lives. And fear is manifested in the form of stress. Once you become aware of this natural process, the fear will have no hold on you and you'll transcend it. The best way to release your fear is to feel and expe-rience it—surrender to the fear and stop fighting it. Just sit with your fear and actually try to melt into it. When you do, some-thing amazing will happen: Your fear will vanish. But remember that fear is nothing more than a feeling—it isn't real. Never run away from your fears; always run toward them. *The place where your greatest fears live is also the place where your greatest growth lies.* And since the purpose of human life is all about growth, embrace the glorious opportunity fear presents. As I mentioned earlier, the things you fear in life offer you a very fertile ground of self-discovery."

"But is it really true that each and every one of us is perceiv-ing our reality in an incorrect way?" I asked.

"I'm not saying that we all see the world incorrectly—some-times we do, but sometimes what we actually think is happen-ing reflects the truth. My point is simply that for your life to change, *you* must change. And one of the best ways to do that is by getting the simple fact that we see the world not as it is, but as we are."

With that, Father Mike led me back to my room and left me alone for the night. My mind was spinning with all I'd learned in the span of such a short period of time. There was so much new information to integrate. Here I was in Rome, being coached by a priest who was sharing with me a view of the uni-verse, one that would revolutionize every area of my life if I adhered to it.

I really did feel fear when I thought about what this incredible monk said. To live my life according to these new beliefs would mean that I'd have to see the world through a completely new set of eyes, and so few people in the world I knew lived like this. Yet as I gazed out over the city and stared at the stars sparkling in that magnificent Roman sky, a peace deeper than anything I'd ever known welled up within me. And a single word flashed across my mind: *trust.*

——— ✦ ———

Over the past few weeks, I'd grown accustomed to a very pleasant routine at the cathedral: waking up at dawn and meditating with Father Mike for about an hour. This discipline was extremely difficult for me at first, but after only a few days, an interior power began to surface within me, and the practice became easier. I started to change even more quickly and started to operate on a whole new level. I began to identify less with my thinking and access a higher level of awareness. The deeper I went, the more I came to see that I was not my thoughts—I was the thinker of my thoughts, and the more I simply became a witness to them, the more my chattering mind would be silenced and stilled.

I knew in my core that I was growing as a human being as I never had before. More than ever, I agreed with Father Mike's view that this path we're all on is not about improving and attempting to become more like someone else, such as our heroes, for instance. Instead, I felt so deeply that this journey of life is really about reclaiming who we truly are. It *is* a process of remembering. But I didn't just believe this—I actually came to *know* this.

After our morning meditation, Father Mike and I would eat a simple breakfast of fruit and grains and then stroll out into the garden behind the cathedral where he'd spend the next few hours coaching me and teaching me the fundamental lessons of living a wise and noble life. On a few of the mornings, he offered his wisdom in the form of sermons, standing next to a beautiful rosebush and speaking with a passion and intensity that connected with the most profound place within my heart. On other days, he'd be more relaxed and make me laugh while he revealed his breathtaking knowledge to me in the form of humorous stories.

Every evening, I'd walk up to my tiny room and open the windows, peering out at the sky and growing in my self-knowledge. Each day I'd have remarkable shifts in the way I saw the world and in my understanding of the design of this gorgeous universe of ours. I quickly came to see that every one of us is connected. There *is* an order to the seemingly random events of our lives, although most of us never recognize this. All the dots in our lives are connected, and everything that happens to us happens for a reason. Life really is a growth school, and each of the circumstances of our lives promote our personal growth if we have the awareness to find and then live by the lesson offered.

Each one of our lives, I realized, has a gracious beauty to it. The sad times improve us and lead us to the good, while the good times show us the fullness of our possibilities and offer us the blessings to be appreciated. And I also realized that nothing very good or very bad ever lasts for very long.

6 THE PURSUIT OF A CAUSE

One morning, Father Mike sat me down on a bench in the lush garden behind the cathedral's back entrance. This was the place where he spent much time in silent contemplation and prayer.

"Keep believing that this universe is a friendly place," he told me. "The world really does want you to win. Let go of the control that most of us live the best years of our lives under, and choose to be curious instead. You'll find that if you live in this way, then a force more powerful than yourself will lead you to your best life on a daily basis. You'll literally be led to your calling."

"I've often wondered what my true mission in life is, Father Mike. Deep down, I've always known that each one of us has something special that we're here to do in the world," I said.

"Here's a big lesson: The secret of passion is purpose. Once you find your calling—that compelling cause that you can give your life over to—your heart will begin to sing, and you'll have more passion, power, and inner peace than you ever could have imagined. Discovering a powerful dream that you can live your life by will give you immense power, drive, and energy. A powerful dream gives you hope, Jack. Focus will flood your days because you'll know exactly what you've been placed on the planet to do."

"Fascinating."

"One of the main reasons to discover and establish a personal vision or a central cause for your life is to focus on your highest priorities. As Edward G. Bulwer-Lytton said: 'The man who succeeds above his fellows is the one who early in life clearly discerns his object and towards that object habitually directs his powers. Even genius itself is but fine observation strengthened by fixity of purpose. Every man who observes vigilantly and resolves steadfastly grows unconsciously into genius.'"

"I've never thought of genius like that," I mused.

"It's all about focusing on your highest goals," Father Mike replied. "When you know what's most important in your life, then you can be more selective about what you do and what you don't do."

"Good point."

"And when you find the primary vocation of your life," he continued, "no adversity will ever hold you back, no matter how severe it is. Articulating a personal vision for your life is the single best way to move through problems and maximize your satisfactions. Da Vinci said it so well when he observed: 'If you fix your course upon a star, you will be able to navigate any storm.'

"You see, Jack, the deepest need of the human heart is the need to live for something higher than ourselves. We all have a deep craving to show up in the world in a way that makes a difference

in the lives of others and connects us with a purpose that tran-
scends the boundaries of our lives. We all have a human hunger to
know at the end of our lives that we haven't walked the planet in
vain. The moment you find your calling, your main aim, your vital
destiny—that's the moment you'll step into a whole new way of
being. You'll stop worrying about making money or being famous
or climbing the corporate ladder, and you'll start concerning yourself with doing your part to create a new world and make it a more
loving place. And that's when the best part within you will start to
feel happy. At a deep level, you'll feel better about yourself as a
human being. You'll start to feel fulfilled, that your life matters.
And this is when your life will takes on the quality of greatness."

"That's fantastic," I replied.

"Let me put it this way: *When you shift from a compulsion to
survive toward a commitment to serve others, your life cannot help but
explode into success.*"

"How do I find this destiny of mine?"

"You really don't discover your destiny, Jack—it discovers
you."

"Really?"

"Yes. The more you recover your authentic self, the more
your destiny will unfold before your eyes. As I told you before,
my young friend, just keep doing your inner work—that's the
most essential thing. As Dutch philosopher Benedict de Spinoza
said: 'To be what we are and to become what we are capable of
being is the only end in life.'" The more you find your essential
self and present it to the world for all to see, the more you'll
move into the flow of life. And by doing so, your destiny will
find you."

I was skeptical. "It's that simple?"

"Yes, actually it is," Father Mike answered. "Just be more
patient and open. Thomas Merton made the point well when he

observed: 'We have what we seek. It is there all the time, and if we give it time it will make itself known to us.' The more you get to know the person that you truly are, the more you'll see that you have all the wisdom, power, and capacity that you've desired all your life. *You already are what you've always dreamed of being.* You just need to know that. And when you do, you'll then be able to access the possibilities that are meant for you. Just keep going deeper and working on yourself. And keep trusting and staying open."

Father Mike paused for a moment, and then went on. "Jack, you've done well here. You've been one of my best students. But our time together is over. You've been with me for four weeks, and the shifts I've seen in you have been wonderful . . . but the best is yet to come. I've planted some seeds within you that have only begun to grow. It's been an honor to meet you, the son of my dear friend Cal. You'll do well in the world and blaze quite a path, I'm sure. Stay true to yourself, Jack. Keep seeking the truth—and always trust."

With that, Father Mike gave me a warm hug. He then briskly turned around and walked through the garden into the cathedral that had been his home for so many years. The sun shone brightly, and I just stood next to a rosebush, reflecting on the past four weeks and what I'd experienced. I thought of the words of Louisa May Alcott:

"Far away there in the sunshine are my highest aspirations.
I may not reach them, but I can look up and see their
beauty, believe in them and try to follow them."

From the place within me that knew, I felt that I was truly on my way.

———— ✦ ————

7 A MEETING WITH A MASTER OF THE HEART

"There is a wick within you that is waiting to become the light of your soul. When this inner flame burns brightly you will feel a magnificent awakening in your life."

— Bradford Keeney

"Every year that I live I am more convinced that the waste of life lies in the love we have not given, the powers we have not used, the selfish prudence which will risk nothing, and which, shirking pain, misses happiness as well."

— Mary Cholmondeley

— ✦ —

My eyes had never seen such a beautiful sight. I'd been to many beaches before, but this one stood out from all the rest. It looked like a tiny slice of Nirvana. And so, as I paid the cab driver, I told him that I'd find a way home.

"Are you sure about that, pal?" he asked. "We're miles from

the nearest town, and this is the most isolated beach on the island. I could come back for you in a few hours if you want."

"No . . . but thanks," I replied. "I have a feeling I'll be fine here. The universe is a friendly place, you know," I added with a knowing smile.

The cabbie just stared at me, shook his head, and drove off.

I couldn't see anyone in sight, but that didn't matter. I slowly made my way down from the road to the sand and took off my sandals. The scene was nothing less than spellbinding: The ocean reflected a brilliant azure blue; the sand was fine and white; and the sun, though strong, caressed my body and filled me with peace. I sat down, giving silent thanks for all the gifts that had begun to fill my life since my meeting with Cal—my father—several weeks before.

After about 20 minutes of joyful sunbathing, I noticed some movement on the far end of the beach. As I concentrated more, I could see what appeared to be a man doing some kind of a tribal dance in the sand. His hands were flailing, his knees were knocking, and his head was shaking. I grew frightened. I was alone here and, for a moment, I questioned my safety. Then something wonderful happened. The word *trust* flashed across my mind, and I remembered what Father Mike had told me one day in Rome: "Behind each of your fears, you'll discover your fortune." I reached deep within myself and found the new sense of courage I'd been accessing more and more of over the past four weeks as I connected to my power. I then boldly began to walk toward the figure.

As I grew closer, I saw the man more clearly. He was still moving oddly, as if in a wild trance, and he didn't seem to notice that he was no longer alone on the beach. Soon I was near him, yet he kept on doing his dance. Finally, he broke the silence and opened his eyes.

"Welcome to my beach, Jack. What took you so long?" he asked with a toothy grin.

I was stunned. How could this man possibly know my name? *Trust* flashed through my mind once again.

"You know my name?" I asked, surprised and still somewhat afraid. "How?"

"Yep, I know your name all right—Cal told me all about you. Quite a guy he was. And boy, could he party."

"You partied with my dad?" I wondered in disbelief.

"Oh, it was all good, clean fun—nothing to worry about," he said, wiping the sweat off his chest.

I studied this mysterious character for a moment while he lifted his face to the sun. I guessed he was about 45 years old. His skin was bronzed and his body was in almost perfect condition, with lean muscles rippling out from beneath his supple skin. His eyes were a striking blue, and his hair was bleached blond from his exposure to the sun. And he only wore a necklace made of seashells and a pair of tattered nylon shorts that seemed to have every color of the rainbow splashed over them.

"My name's Moe. Moe Jackson," he said as he extended his hand. "Welcome to Hawaii. This is my beach—best place on the island to surf, and I've got it all to myself. The locals say it's haunted out here, so there's no chance of any company. Fine by me," he drawled. "I get to surf out here all day, all by myself, which suits me perfectly."

"You're a surfer?" I asked.

"You got it, brother," he replied joyfully. "Just like Cal. He was pretty darn good at it, too—almost as good as me," he grinned.

"And what about that thing you were just doing? That little jig?"

"Oh, I was just havin' some fun. I love to dance—it keeps me in the flow of life and reminds me not to take things too seriously."

"In the flow of life?"

"Sure," Moe said. "I live my life moment to moment. I'm dedicated to living in a state of continuous grace. I try to stay completely present to everything that unfolds for me. The past is over—long gone. So my philosophy works like this: I never let my yesterdays take up much of my todays."

"And what about the future?" I questioned.

"The future isn't real, man. It's just an illusion as far as I'm concerned. The only thing that I really focus on is the enchantment of each minute. I live in the flow and take things as they come. I follow my heart. And I love it!" he offered with immense enthusiasm. "Here, this is for you," he added as he handed me an envelope that he took from the pocket of his shorts. "Read the page inside."

I pulled out a crumpled piece of paper and read its words carefully. It said:

> *"Normal day, let me be aware of the treasure you are. Let me not pass you by in quest of some rare and perfect tomorrow. One day I shall dig my nails into the earth, or bury my face in my pillow or stretch myself taut or raise my hands to the sky and want, more than all the world, your return."*
>
> — Mary Jean Iron

"I guess that's true," I said reflectively. "So many of us complain about not having enough time in our lives, and yet we waste much of the time we already have. And we spend our lives chasing this elusive pot of gold, only to discover that our best treasures were the simplest ones that we always had but never knew."

"You got it," Moe said, nodding his head in agreement. "Most people are always running toward this fantasyland that they think will solve all their problems and fill them up with joy. They tell themselves, 'Once I achieve this or that, I'll be happy.' But I believe that happiness isn't a place you get to—it's an inner state you create. *Anyone* can be happy—it's available to everyone and is available right now. We just need to stop and pay more attention to the treasures that already surround us. So now I live my life full out. My eyes are open. I've awakened. I love every single moment of this grand adventure."

"And where do you live?" I asked with curiosity.

He pointed to a tiny thatched hut at the edge of the beach, where the shore jutted out like a finger. There was a small garden filled with flowers next to it, and a rusty old bicycle leaning against the side.

"That's my palace, Jack, my home. And I love it!" he proclaimed proudly.

"Interesting," I replied, not quite knowing what to think.

"It's more than interesting—it's perfect. I've got nothing to worry about, no one to bother me, and I'm next to those waves that make my heart pound. I'm in heaven as far as I'm concerned. So welcome to paradise! This will be your home for the next four weeks."

"Sounds great to me. I know I'm in for a real treat," I answered with a smile.

"It's all been planned for you," Moe continued. You already know that, I'm sure. And I'll be happy to have the gift of your company. I'll be teaching you all about the second of The Final Questions."

"Did I love well?" I recalled.

"You got it."

"Great. But right now, Moe, to be completely candid with

you, I need to focus on my inner work more than falling in love. I'm going through so much internal growth that every element of my life seems to be changing. My whole stained glass window is transforming, so to speak."

"Father Mike taught you that, I know. Brilliant man," Moe said sincerely.

"You know Father Mike?"

"Of course. He's been a friend for years—scared of the water, though," my companion noted with a chuckle. "I could never get him near a surfboard, no matter how hard I tried. His loss," he shrugged.

"Anyway, to respond to your point," Moe continued, "there are many types of love: erotic love, self-love, love of family, and love of life itself and its miraculous unfolding. The last of these is what you and I will be focusing on, my friend. Our work together will be all about opening up your heart so you can then open up to life and all its delights. I'll bet you never dreamed of having a personal heart coach, right?"

"A heart coach? Never heard of it."

"Yeah, I know," said Moe. "It's a little corny, but Cal wanted it that way. He set up all this life training for you and asked us to be your coaches. He really wanted to help you, Jack—the guy truly loved you. But let me continue. I've found a way to live a life that's rich and amazing. I mean *really* rich and *really* amazing. I'm the happiest guy I know, here on this empty beach. I wake up every morning with deep joy in my heart. I surf. I dance. I paint during the morning, and sometimes late at night, I watch the stars as I fall asleep. I write poetry as the sun sets. I feel I'm the richest man in the world. And the beautiful thing is that I'm really no different from you. You can have what I have—if you want it."

Moe went on. "It all happened when I stopped living my

days in my head and begin to open my heart. That's been the real trick for me. Carl Jung said it best: 'Your vision will become clear only when you look into your heart. Who looks outside, dreams. Who looks inside, awakens.'"

"Great line," I said, feeling a wave of peace and comfort wash over me as I took in those words. "Well, it's wonderful to meet you, Moe Jackson. I'm genuinely looking forward to our time together," I expressed with utter confidence.

"Great!" he said. "Jack, I hear you when you say that you're in a period of deep transformation. That's good—best place to be in life. I know it can be terrifying at times, but just hang in there. Try to be fully present in this process you're going through. It's the most important time of your life . . . so far. So just ride this wave—you'll be glad you did. In fact, I'll bet that after your stay with Father Mike, your heart is already starting to open up to your inner wisdom."

"You're right. I'm getting all these insights I've never had before—and I'm not really sure where they're coming from," I noted, hoping for some guidance.

"You're getting out of your head and moving into your heart, which is where all your answers live. Living in your head is playing it safe with your life. You try to figure things out. You plan and worry and fret about your past, your present, and your future. You spend so much time analyzing what could be and what would be that you miss out on living the life that you need to live. The ideal way to learn from life is to be present to every moment presented to you—and you can't do that if you're caught up in your thoughts."

Moe stopped for a second, and then continued. "I used to be like you, Jack, living in my mind. I actually used to be in the same industry you're in."

"Advertising?"

"Yes, advertising. Ever heard of MJ Group International?"

"Of course. They're one of the top-five ad agencies in the world. Based in Chicago, 23 offices around the world, hundreds of millions of dollars in annual revenues."

"Guess who founded that baby?" Moe asked as he patted himself on his back lightheartedly.

"Don't tell me!" I replied. "MJ is you, Moe Jackson?"

"Yes." He beamed.

"Unbelievable. Really?" I couldn't believe that this surfer I was casually chatting with had been one of the most famous marketing minds in the world only a decade ago. His firm had pioneered many innovations and was widely known for its ruthless tactics and win-at-all-costs mind-set. MJ International was a world-class company, and it was difficult to fathom that this extraordinarily peaceful-looking man standing in front of me on this gorgeous beach in the middle of nowhere was who he said he was.

"Trust me, it's true," Moe replied. "My ride to success was a fast one. I seemed to have the Midas touch when I was in the business. I was unstoppable for many years, making millions in the process. I just had this sixth sense about how to get ahead. By the age of 40, I had most of the material possessions that any person from your world could ever dream of: a private jet, a home in the Caymans, a place in Aspen, a couple of hot Porsches in the driveway, and a trophy wife. And after all those years spent chasing money, fame, and acclaim, guess what I discovered?"

"Tell me," I asked as I looked deep into Moe's eyes, which had become filled with a look of sadness and regret.

"I learned that I still saw the same person in the mirror every morning. I still felt the same way I had when I was hungry and broke. I still had the same demons plaguing me and the same baggage I'd hauled around with me since I was a kid. I still had the same limiting beliefs about myself and what I could be. So I learned that no matter how beautiful your outer world looks, it's what's on the inside that's important. And if your inner world is messy and unhealthy, nothing that you get on the outside will ever make you happy. On the other hand, if your inner world is healthy and complete, the simplest and most basic of things in your outer world will fill your heart and soul. The greatest treasures of life truly are the inner ones, my friend. As Emerson noted: 'Without the rich heart, wealth is an ugly beggar.'"

"I'm learning that as I go deep," I added reflectively.

"No matter how much we collect, nothing—nothing—can ever make up for any incompleteness we feel within ourselves. As human beings, we all have these holes within us that crave to be filled. Some of us have holes created by parents who didn't care for our emotional needs as children; others of us have holes created by uncaring schoolmates who couldn't see our true worth. Still others of us have holes created by educators who taught us that we were never good enough, no matter how much we achieved. And as we grow into adults, we unconsciously look for other people and things to fill our holes—to complete us. And when they don't, we move on in search of the next solution. It's an endless pursuit, and it empties us—as human beings—of our inner peace."

"So what's the lasting solution?" I asked as Moe and I strolled along the beach, with a gentle breeze caressing our faces.

"Go within," came the reply. "Do whatever it takes to complete yourself. Fill your own holes. And remember that the gateway to fulfillment swings inward, not outward. That's why the first priority of every human being, as far as I can tell, is to do the deep inside stuff, the inner work you just spoke of."

"That's a fascinating way to look at it, Moe."

"It's true. Going within means that you address the things that are limiting you from knowing how fantastic you truly are."

"Such as my incorrect beliefs, false assumptions, fears, and personal biases," I piped in.

"Yes, those things and more. By dealing with these things in a very real way, you then can feel much better in your external world. The more you clean up your inner world, the more beautiful your outer world will be."

"It all begins within," I summarized.

"Yes," Moe said. "And one of the main elements of that inner work is to open up the heart. Opening up your heart is about living with love—being open to human possibilities, trusting in the perfect unfolding of your life, and being more alive. Begin to live in the wonder of your life, Jack—be present to all of the brilliance around you. It really is a choice you have the power to make. And with a little practice, you'll master these skills. As Helen Keller said: 'No pessimist ever discovered the secrets of the stars, or sailed to an uncharted land, or opened a new heaven to the human spirit.' Be more courageous with your life—that's what worked for me. Opening your heart is also about trusting your instincts more often and being open to the surprises that weave in and out of our lives. It's about welcoming the unexpected and being available for all the miracles that have been awaiting you."

"I don't know if I believe in miracles. I'm more open to things than ever before, but believing in miracles is a stretch for me," I admitted.

Just then, Moe began to run. At first it was more of a jog, but then he began to sprint. "Follow me!" he instructed.

I began to run, too, giving myself over to this experience and trusting that some lesson would come from it.

Moe led the way along the beach for what seemed like 15 or

20 minutes, all the while remaining silent and staying focused on his goal: a sandy hilltop at the very end of the beach. Finally, as he approached his destination, I caught up with him. Sweat streamed down my cheeks, and I struggled to catch my breath.

"Too much of that rich Italian food, I can see," joked Moe as he pointed the way to the path up the hill.

"Where are we going?" I gasped.

"You'll see," he replied.

At the top of the hill was a lush, grassy mound. From this perch, I could see other islands, passing steamships, and strikingly beautiful coral formations.

"Look over there," said Moe as he pointed to what appeared to be ancient ruins a little way off into the distance.

"What are those?" I asked.

"Well," responded Moe as he played with one of the shells on his exotic necklace, "at first glance they probably look like historical ruins or a rudimentary series of walls and roadways. But I'll tell you something really cool about what you're looking at. If you were to fly high above these ruins—which were created by the earliest inhabitants of Hawaii many, many years ago—you'd discover something that scientific researchers found out recently as they surveyed this site from helicopters and airplanes."

"I'm all ears," I said eagerly.

"What appears to be a random series of paths and walls is actually a sophisticated and enormously complex series of highways and systems that lay at the foundation of a rich civilization when viewed from a higher, more complete perspective.

"The point is really this," Moe explained. "When you see things from a higher perspective, you can see that seemingly unrelated things are actually related. And to me, that's a miracle. You see, a miracle is nothing more than a shift of mind that helps you see things in a new way. By going up to this hilltop, you can see things differently than you would down on the ground. And by constantly staying open to viewing your life in new ways, you'll eventually see the miracles that *are* taking place. The more open you remain, the more you'll see that all of the seemingly unrelated things that have happened to you during your life have been part of a larger coherent system. This is what I see as a miracle."

Moe then dropped to the ground. Within seconds, he was doing push-ups at a furious pace.

"What the heck are you doing now?" I asked with surprise.

"Just keepin' in shape," he replied.

He continued his teaching as sweat poured down his forehead. "Jack, there's so much more waiting for you out there than you ever could have guessed. The key is to trust."

There was that word again. I knew I had to trust that everything that had happened to me in the past, and that all that would happen to me in the future was part of a perfectly orchestrated program to lead me along the path of my destiny and highest truth.

"Stop living in your head," Moe said. "You've tried that method of operating your whole life, and where has it gotten you?"

"I'm still stuck, even after all these years," I admitted.

"Maybe it's time for a new operating system, to live more of your moments out of your heart. *Be* more love, and I promise that the golden gates to a whole new world will open up for you. Once you begin living your life fully from the deepest place within you and loving who you are, all things will change for the better. *Live your life as a meditation on love*—love of others, love for yourself, and love for the world. That's what I'm really saying."

"So how did you end up here? What's your story, Moe?"

"We all have a story, don't we? Well, I eventually decided to drop out of my life because it grew out of control. I gave away everything I owned and traveled the world with a backpack for a few years. I met fascinating people and immersed myself in various cultures. I went to personal-growth seminars and spent months alone in the wilderness. I learned to meditate in India and fell in love with surfing in Australia. As I did more and more work on myself, I came to a point where I began to find answers to the biggest questions of my life. I began to evolve into an entirely new person in many ways. Then on a visit to this incredible island, I discovered this beach. In doing so, I found my home. I just felt that this is where I belonged. And I've been here ever since."

"Incredible." I thought for a moment, and then asked, "Is it important to be alone to find oneself?"

"No, not at all," Moe responded. "Actually, being alone for long periods of time might actually be a form of running away from what needs to be looked at. It almost might be a kind of distraction from going deep into what really needs to be dealt with. When I was in India, I saw many monks who I heard spend the best years of their lives alone, up in the mountains, with nothing more that a loincloth and a rice bowl as their possession. I never thought those people were all that enlightened."

"That surprises me."

"Well, it's pretty easy to be peaceful sitting alone on a mountaintop with nothing to do but contemplate your thoughts. It isn't hard to be happy and stress free all day when you're all by yourself and there's no one around to press your buttons and bring up your deeper issues. To me, growth comes from being in the real world. We discover who we are as people in relationship to others. In my experience, I've found that it's only when we surround ourselves with other people that we know over true selves. I'll give you a metaphor. Let's say that you found yourself completely alone in a white box. There are no windows or doors—just you."

"Okay, I'm visualizing this," I said with both eyes closed.

"Good. Now do you see what I'm getting at? Without anything else to view yourself against, you can't really know much about yourself. It's just you alone in the box."

"I see exactly what you're getting at. I need another thing in that box for me to compare myself to."

"Well, I don't know if *compare* is the correct word, but you're on the right track. If I put a surfboard in that white box with you, there would now be a relationship in play. You could look at the board and then look at yourself. There would now be a way you could get information about yourself, relative to the surfboard—in relation to it. You might notice that you're taller than the board, or more intelligent, or that you move more. So it's only in relationship that we come to know ourselves."

"Very cool point," I replied.

"Bring that metaphor into the discussion about the monk and the rice bowl. Up on the mountaintop, he isn't in relationship. And given this, there's no real growth and self-discovery. But the moment we bring him back to the real world . . . " Moe trailed off.

"He's in relationship to other people," I interjected. "He can see himself against others in the world."

"Yes. And as he goes through his days, the highs and lows of the world cause him to respond in certain ways. If someone treats him poorly, he may get mad. The anger that surfaces is nothing more than an opportunity to heal a deeper wound. If something frightens him, this is another chance to learn something more about himself, and in doing so, raise his consciousness to the next level. If a challenge he experiences frustrates him, then this raises yet another vehicle for him to bring it all back to himself and seek out what within him needs to be strengthened and improved. If a challenge he experiences frustrates him, this raises yet another vehicle for him to bring it all back to himself and seek out what within him needs to be strengthened and improved. Do you see how living in the real world, going to work, paying bills, and essentially experiencing the human condition is the only way to move toward enlightenment?"

"I do. I get it clearly. But then, and I hope you don't mind me asking this, why are *you* living all alone?"

Moe fell silent. After pondering my question for a few moments, he smiled. "That's a great point. I don't know the answer to that one, Jack. All I can say is that I know that I'm exactly where I'm supposed to be. I've lived in the world my whole life, and now my path has led me to this place. My intention is to remain here, but our lives unfold in ways well beyond what we expect. Who knows where I'll be a year from now? I'm enjoying where I am right now. I'm just playing in the present moment, open to all possibilities and potentials. My heart feels so happy here. And until it tells me otherwise, this is where I'll be."

I wasn't quite satisfied with Moe's answer, but I didn't call him on it. This man with the look of an Adonis and the peace of the Buddha clearly knew something I didn't. There was no doubt in my mind that he was living his life according to a philosophy that was far more enlightened than mine.

Until I met Father Mike only a few weeks ago, my life was a mess. By embracing his unique wisdom, my life was flying forward. Who was I to judge the way Moe lived? Yes, his approach was unconventional. But if we all only lived according to the conventional thinking of the masses, our society would have remained in the Dark Ages. It's only due to the novel and bold thinking of the visionaries of our world that any progress has been made. And on top of that, what Moe was teaching made sense.

"Jack, I've shared a ton of knowledge with you today—I hope it's been helpful," Moe said. "But we'll have lots to discuss over the next month. And while you're here, you'll be staying in my guest house."

"Guest house?" I wondered aloud, not seeing any structure other than his hut on the beach.

"Yeah—it's over there," came the reply as Moe pointed to an old bed with a wooden frame that sat just behind his "palace."

"You'll be sleeping under the stars while you're here in Hawaii. It'll be great for you." With that, Moe climbed down onto the beach, grabbed his surfboard, and hit the waves.

8

WALKING
INTO THE MYSTERY

"That it will never come again is what makes life so sweet."

— Emily Dickinson

———— ✦ ————

As Moe and I ate a breakfast of papaya and oranges on the sand the next morning, I was bursting with curiosity. So I asked him if he could share some specifics on the subject of the heart.

"My life was transformed when I began to follow my heart," he began. "It's so important to follow your heart because it contains a higher intelligence than that contained within your head. Accessing the wisdom of the heart connects you with the larger wisdom of the world and opens up a doorway into the heart of the universe. I don't mean to sound too mystical, but that's what I've found to be true. I totally trust the wisdom my heart offers to me."

"So I need to *live* in my heart?"

"No, it's actually a balance—a partnership. To live your highest life, as best as I can tell, the trick is to have the heart and the mind working together in harmony. Some people live completely in their hearts—they're pure emotion and feeling. These people often have trouble operating in the real world, appearing as love-struck fools with poor judgment and no practical awareness. Other people live totally in their heads—they're all reason and logic, leaving no room for intuition and passion to guide them."

"Kind of like Mr. Spock on the old *Star Trek* television show."

"Yes, Jack, that's a good example. And like Spock, such individuals appear cold as stone. My belief is that life's all about striking a balance: Get the head and the heart working as teammates, as life partners. Live in a way that's wise yet kind, practical yet spontaneous, courageous yet caring, responsible yet passionate. It takes effort and time to get this balance right—I still struggle with it myself on many days. But with commitment and patience, it will all come."

"How can I open up my heart, Moe? I really want to *feel* more and discover the joy in life, to live with more festivity and happiness," I said. "My sense is that my life will open once my heart does—just as you say—but telling me to open my heart is a little like asking me to chat with you in Hawaiian. I don't know where to start."

"I hear you completely," replied Moe with what I felt was genuine empathy. "I experienced the same thing as I journeyed along my path. And that's why I'm the perfect coach for you, if you don't mind my saying so. We teach what we most need to learn, and the biggest lesson of my life has been making the gifts of my heart more available to myself. And I've learned so much that I can share with you. In fact, I'm reminded of an old story about what lies within the heart. May I share it with you?"

"Go for it."

"In the East, many thousands of years ago, it was believed

that every person on Earth was a god. But humankind abused their powers, so the Supreme Lord decided that he'd take it all away. The question then became where he would hide the godhead—the source of all human talent, potential, and glory. The first advisor said, 'Why don't you dig a hole deep in the ground and place the godhead in there?' 'No,' replied the master, 'eventually someone will dig deep enough and find it.' The second advisor then spoke. 'I have an idea,' he said. 'Why not put this source of all human power on the top of the highest mountain?' Again the master refused. 'No. Someone will eventually scale that mighty mountain and find it.' Finally, the third advisor commented, 'What if you place the godhead at the bottom of the world's deepest ocean?' The master replied, 'No, someone will dive down into the ocean and discover it.' The master then paused and reflected. After a few moments, he spoke knowingly: 'I have the solution. I will place this source of extraordinary power, magnificence, and glory inside the heart of every man, woman, and child on the planet, for they'll never think to look there.'"

"That's a great story," I said.

"You see, Jack, your heart contains a lot more wisdom and gifts than you give it credit for. You may think your mind has all the answers—that if you could just think more, you'll have more. You might imagine that if you simply gathered more information and learned more, you'd win at the game of life. And you may believe that if you could just figure out what's not working in your life, you'd know how to get things working again. But I don't think that's how life works."

"I need to shift into my heart a little more?" I guessed.

"A lot more," Moe stated in a relaxed tone. "But please be gentle with yourself. The path from head to heart is not a short one. It may take weeks, months, or even years for you to completely open up. The main thing is that you get on the path."

"And exactly how do I do that?"

"You're on the path now," Moe replied. "The very fact that you've been brave enough to come here and seek me out shows me that the place within you that knows is ready for your broken heart to be healed."

I knew what Moe meant when he referred to my broken heart. I feel that everyone in this world of ours has had a broken heart at some time or another. I'm not just referring to the broken heart that occurs when we lose someone we love—I mean the breaking of our hearts that happens when we begin to realize that our dreams have faded and our deepest longings have never been fulfilled, when we see the current state of our world and the less-than-loving values that run it, and when we sell ourselves short in life and minimize our destinies. I thought about what Benjamin Disraeli once said: "Life is too short to be little."

Moe continued to speak. "This beach is a good metaphor for your life, Jack. Life is a beach in so many ways. It reflects a journey that has its sandy parts as well as its rocky areas, and it has its curves and its straightaways. Sometimes you see the crashing waves when you wake up in the morning and feel the fury of the ocean; other times there's a blissful calm and not a thing stirs. As I've lived my life out on this beach, I've come to understand that the laws of life are really nothing more than the laws of nature. Study the way nature operates and you can figure out how life, at its truest level, works."

Father Mike had taught me this as well.

"I'll give you an example," said Moe. "I've spent many nights alone out here on this beach. Sometimes I'll stay up all night, just breathing and thinking and soaking up the majesty of this place. It never ceases to amaze me how the brightness of the dawn always comes immediately after the darkest part of the night. And that's the same in our lives. Each and every one of us has to endure darkness—but it *always* passes, and the light always returns. It's actually at the moment when you're most into your problems that you're closest to your solutions. And when you're experiencing the deepest pain, your greatest peace is running toward you."

I'd never thought of life with this perspective before. Moe's wisdom had a certain grace and elegance about it and was similar to the teachings Father Mike had so lovingly shared with me—both spoke to an extraordinary intelligence of the world we live in. According to both of these masters, each human being's life seemed to unfold according to a precise plan—everything happened for a reason, and life was nothing less than a miraculous gift.

"Let me give you some practical advice now, Jack. One of the first things you can do to reconnect with your heart is to rekindle the passions that have died within you. Start doing the things that, in the past, filled up that big heart of yours. Begin to do what speaks to the passionate kid within you and makes you laugh so hard your belly hurts. Rediscover the things that move you and bring tears to your eyes—after all, the place where tears are brought to your eyes is the place where the universe wants you to be."

"I wonder why it's taken me so long to get to the point where I'm ready to experience a love for life itself. To be honest with you, Moe, I feel bad that it's taken me so many years," I said as my gaze fell down to the sand, and regret welled up within me.

"Stop beating yourself up, Jack. It's like I told you earlier—you're exactly where you're supposed to be. Stop questioning your path, and enjoy the place you've come to. Everything that's happened to you along the way was meant to be. Acceptance is the key here. *Now* is a special time in your life—savor it. You're getting your original life back—the one that was meant for you before other things got in the way."

Suddenly Moe's face broke out into a huge grin. "It's time for you to have fun in life again," he said. "When I was a kid, my mother and father used to tell me that my eyes shined. They'd tell me that there actually was a twinkle in them. Now I see what they were saying: A child at play has eyes that shine."

"Well, I used to be a pretty excited little kid, too."

"I want you to get that twinkle back. And as you do, your heart will open more and begin to whisper its truth to you."

"I'd love for that to happen, Moe."

"And it will. My advice to you is to begin to do more of the things that make you the happiest. Follow your bliss, and start doing more of the things that made your heart sing in the past. As we grow older, we lose sight of the things that used to make our pulses quicken."

"I can't even remember what my passions were anymore," I sadly admitted.

"No problem. They'll find you again once you start seeking them out," Moe reassured me. "Ask yourself questions, for the very act of engaging in creative self-questioning will elicit many of the answers you're seeking. Ask yourself questions such as, 'What did I do in the past that made me feel good about myself?' or 'If I didn't have to work, how would I spend my days?' And I also suggest that you begin to listen a lot more."

"To what?"

"To those inner calls, Jack. Pay more attention to those silent and gentle promptings that speak from the deepest places within you. They're there, they have a voice, and they're crying out to be heard. You knew them when you were a kid—get to know them again as an adult."

"I'm so detached from this kind of thing that I'm afraid I've lost any kind of a connection to this deeper part of myself. I know I'm shut down, and I really do live in my head. But I'm willing to start listening for these inner calls you speak of."

"Wonderful," Moe replied. "Your intention to begin listening to your heart more is a giant step toward opening it and benefiting from the enormous gifts it has to give you. Intentions alone are like huge waves that cascade throughout the universe, and they inevitably return bearing wonderful presents. Just keep listening and observing.

"Jack, remember that our hearts speak to us in the silent spaces of our lives. Make time to reflect and sit with things. And trust that a time will come when all the changes you're hoping for will appear in your life."

"The universe is a friendly place," I added, repeating what had become a mantra of sorts for me as I journeyed into the uncharted waters of my life.

"You got it, brother. By trusting that it will all work out okay, then no matter what happens, your new reality will move toward you. It's like what the Sufi poet Rumi said so many years ago: 'Keep knocking and the joy inside will eventually open a window and look out to see who's there.' These promptings will lead you in certain directions—they're the voices of your heart guiding you in the direction of your destiny. Have the courage to stand in the mystery of your life, and you'll be advancing nicely along your path."

"Live in the mystery? That's a pretty neat way to put it, Moe."

"Well, I've found in my life that the only thing you can really count on in life is the unexpected. The magic that is your life awakens when you jump into the mystery of it all. We should all spend more time in the fantasy that our lives were meant to be. I love the words of T. H. Huxley, which speak to this point: 'Sit down before fact like a little child and be prepared to give up every preconceived notion. Follow humbly wherever and whatever abyss nature leads, or you shall learn nothing.'"

With that, Moe sat down on the beach and motioned for me to join him. He began to build an elaborate sand castle, complete with turrets and a bridge fashioned from a shell. He worked silently for some time. Finally, he continued our discussion. "Our hearts want us to be free," he said as he put the finishing touches on his work of art. "One of the biggest desires of our hearts is for us to be explorers, traveling through life with a sense of wonder and awe—but it won't happen if we're closed to the possibilities of life. We really do need to give up all of our preconceived notions of what our lives must look like and what it will take for us to be happy. I really do try to 'follow humbly wherever and whatever nature leads me to.' Who am I to play God with my life?"

"What a profound statement, Moe. You've obviously done a lot of thinking on this subject."

"A lot of feeling is more like it," was the reply. "An even more profound statement on this point comes from Albert Einstein, who once observed: 'The most beautiful thing we can experience is the mysterious. It is the source of all true art and science. He to whom this emotion is a stranger, who can no longer pause to wonder and stand rapt in awe, is as good as dead; his eyes are closed.'"

"So we're most fully alive when we're living with a sense of wonder and awe. Sounds like a very free way to live," I said. "Just open up to the mystery of it all. I think I could do that."

"This way of operating as a human being will bring up your fears from time to time—that's only natural. But feel those fears, and then do it anyway. Just stand with your fears and let them wash through you. Eventually they'll pass. Here's the real key on this point: *For your life to be great, your faith must be bigger than your fears.* It's only when you have faith in the fact that, as you say, the universe is a friendly place and it's bigger than the fears that have limited you—only then will your brightest life come calling. Your faith in the fact that this world has your best interests in mind but often send its miracles disguised as difficulties must be far bigger than your fear of those difficulties ruining your life. Your faith in the intelligence of the universe must be a lot larger than your fears that you're all alone. There's a much bigger plan unfolding, and you must trust in it. Once you do, the enchantment of your life will be given permission to rise to the surface."

Moe scratched his stomach and stretched a little. "Anyway, back to my point about recovering your passions," he said. "When we grow up in environments where there isn't a lot of personal autonomy—in other words, when we're told what to do all the time—we lose touch with the true desires of our hearts. We lose that connection with our preferences and the things that make our hearts sing. We lose a sense of what we love, and then we grow into adults who don't even know what our true desires are. Consequently, we don't know how to get our hearts beating and savor that experience of being fully alive, engaged, and in the now. And so, our true passions become buried within us."

"Buried?"

"Yes. I don't know if you know this, Jack, but the respected painter James McNeill Whistler studied at West Point Military Academy. While he was in an engineering class, the teacher asked the students to draw a picture of a bridge. Whistler drew a marvelous image of a stone-arched bridge and placed two happy young boys fishing on it. The instructor saw the two children, grew annoyed, and angrily instructed Whistler to remove them from the bridge. Whistler redrew the sketch, this time placing the boys on the river bank. The teacher grew even more agitated and screamed at Whistler to remove the children from the picture entirely. Whistler did so, but in the final version of the sketch, he replaced the figures of the two boys with something that made the teacher shudder."

"What did Whistler do?"

"He drew two small tombstones along the river's edge that had the children's names on them."

"I get the point of wisdom," I said. "When we lose our connection to our hearts, we essentially lose the connection to that spirited child within us."

"Yes, Jack. And it takes real practice to reconnect with those things that speak to us most deeply and recover our childlike spark. It takes a lot of work to get back to knowing who we truly are."

"What kind of work?"

"Once again, it's inner work. Start by reflecting daily on the kinds of things make you happy. For instance, what pursuits energize you and put a smile on your face? Write all this down, as noting your reflections on paper deepens your understanding of them. These are the longings of your heart that *must* be fulfilled if you hope to create an extraordinary life. To use the words of Joseph Campbell: 'If you do follow your bliss, you put yourself on a kind of track that has been there all the while, waiting for you, and the life that you ought to be living is the one you are living. When you see that, you begin to meet people who are in the field of your bliss, and they open the doors to you. I say follow your bliss and don't be afraid, and doors will open where you didn't know they were going to be.'"

"That's an incredibly rich statement," I observed.

"It is. When you follow the longings of your heart and listen to the desires of your true self, a universe of possibilities will open up and you'll step through a doorway into a completely new reality. Meaningful coincidences will begin to occur—for example, the right job will come along at the right time. You'll seem to have an almost magic touch, attracting the right people and the best opportunities into your life. But these kinds of happenings will be nothing more than confirmation from the world that you're now on your authentic path."

As Moe was speaking, a huge waved crashed against a collage of rocks and sprayed us with the freshness of the ocean. I felt irritated rather than exhilarated, but Moe began to laugh.

"Whoooeeee, that felt good. Hit me with some more of that!" he yelled to the ocean without a hint of self-consciousness. He then continued his sharing. "It's also really important to stop the struggle," he remarked.

"What do you mean by that?" I inquired.

"Stop struggling and start being. Struggle breeds stress, and stress is a great barrier to living in a state of grace, ease, and flow—the kind of state you need to be in to attract your best life to you. When I was in the corporate world, all I saw were people struggling, pushing, and trying. There was too much *doing* and not enough *being*. The laws of nature don't work that way. To grow a flower, there's no struggle or trying—it just happens. It's a lovely, natural unfolding that takes place. To try to push the flower to grow just kills the thing. And yet that's what we're inclined to do in our lives. You can't push the ocean, Jack. You need to let it flow. And if you don't get this point and you stay in the struggle, you're basically going against the rules of nature."

"And that's asking for trouble, I assume?"

"Well, I don't know if I'd word it so strongly, but I'd say that in going against the rules of nature, you'll definitely set yourself up for a lesson or two."

"Agreed."

"So all I'm saying is flow through life more, man. And then life will flow through you. Live in a state of calm surrender, going with what life has in store for you. Stop fighting your life, making your happiness conditional on things looking a certain way. Ironically, when you do so, your life will begin to improve and true happiness will flow to you. Stop trying to analyze every event as good or bad and just experience it. That's the path to mastery: detachment from outcomes. Don't let the best hours of your life escape you. Get out of the struggle and get into the energy that really runs the world. The same energy that created that powerful ocean out there created you, too. So, rather than fight it, unite with it—stop trying so hard to get what you want in life. That's one of the paradoxes of the world: Those things that you run toward will run away from you. The more you stop worrying about the way your life should turn out, the more your life will turn out just fine."

"Okay, Moe, I get it. I guess I need to stop living the frantic life I've been living. I need to get out of the struggle of it all and just be with all that's unfolding—knowing that I'm exactly where I'm meant to be. I guess what you're really telling me is that I should stop trying to run my life and just embrace it, trusting that no matter what it currently looks like, it's all part of a grander plan for me."

"Yes. Your life, my life, every life is so beautiful. We just fail to make the time to take that in. That's why it's so important to slow down. Why are you always rushing? Where are you running to?"

"I've never really thought about it. But you're quite right. Until a few weeks ago, my life was nothing more than one long race. The funny thing is that I'm beginning to realize that I didn't even know where the finish line was. I was running just for the sake of running. Maybe I was trying to be so busy to look important."

Moe nodded. "That was probably part of it."

"I think I was also doing it to complete myself and fill in one of those internal holes you spoke of."

"Probably. But the point is really this, Jack: Enjoy the process, the grand unfolding of your life. Become more present to your life—show up more fully and savor the moments. That's all that really matters. The road is better than the end."

Moe was right. Life was nothing more than a series of moments. If I missed them, I'd miss out on life. It was time for me to change in a big way. "Now when it comes to working on myself as a human being, shouldn't I work hard and fast so I can change as quickly as possible?"

"Nice question. Again I'll ask, 'What's the rush?' Life's a process, Jack. And it's also full of paradoxes. Here's another one: By going too fast, you'll actually slow down your progress."

"Father Mike taught me the same thing."

"Well, he was right. Rushing your personal transformation will move you backwards. You need to give your learning some breathing space. Learn, do, and then *be*—that's the master's path."

"Learn, do, and then *be?*"

"Yes. In learning any skill, especially the skill of living a life based on loving your journey and living in the moment, there's a three-step process to get to mastery. First you learn what you need to learn, which might be accomplished by reading the right books about the skill you aim to master. Then you need to allow the learning to settle in and integrate within your life. This happens by *experiencing* what you've learned in the laboratory of your days. That's the 'do' part of the formula. Once that happens, and it might take a long time, you'll eventually get to the 'being' part of your life. That's where the masters live. They don't try to live, they just live. And they don't try to be fully present, they just are."

"Really interesting ideas you have, Moe. Simply profound in so many ways."

"And profoundly simple. I'll tell you another way to express what I've just taught you. There are four stages that one must pass through in moving from living like a beginner to living like a master. The first is *unconscious incompetence*. Sadly, this is where most people spend their lives. In this introductory stage, we don't know what we don't know. We're essentially unconscious—we're asleep to who we truly are and what our lives could become. But once we open our eyes and wake up by taking some responsibility for our lives and the creation of our destinies, we rise to the second stage, which is *conscious incompetence*. Here, we develop a sense of awareness about what we don't know."

"In other words, we become conscious of our incompetence in the way we run our lives?"

"Exactly. Once here, if we stay conscious and keep doing the inside work to open up, we'll get to the next stage: *conscious competence*. This place is characterized by wonderful results starting to appear in life. We're consciously creating an extraordinary existence. The only problem is that we're still trying. There's still struggle."

"And that breeds stress," I interjected.

"Right. We're consciously competent in the way we conduct your life. That's a good place to be, but not a truly great place to live. We all should aspire to get to the final and highest stage—

unconscious competence. This stage in life is the stage of mastery. And it's not about learning any longer or doing any more—it's simply about being."

"I understand," I said. "I love the way you explain the process. So, in many ways, that's the journey of life that we should all aspire to?"

"For me it is. Anyway, all that's important for you to know now is to be cool. Relax, man. 'Hang loose,' as we say here in Hawaii. 'Perfect speed, my son, is being there,' said the wise author Richard Bach. It's time to 'be there' in your life again."

Moe then walked into his "palace" and brought out a lunch of tuna sandwiches and more fresh fruit. We ate silently for what seemed like an hour, just taking in the beauty of this dazzling place of nature and enjoying the sun kissing our faces.

"Yes, living in your head and away from your heart is a pretty stressful way to go, my friend," Moe finally said, still looking out at the ocean. "It's not an elegant way to live. There's a better way to experience your life's path. Maybe the best way to put it is like this: Shift from trying to control your life to becoming curious about your life."

"And what exactly does that mean?"

"Rather than trying to know and figure it all out, live in the curiosity of it all. You don't have to know where you'll be a year from now—you don't even have to know what you'll be doing a month from now. Move away from this need for certainty that we all have, and move toward the curiosity that we all need. Just be. Live in the moment with every bit of your life force, and enjoy the gift of the present. The treasures of your life will present themselves to you only if you really are open to them."

"But surely you aren't saying that there's no need to ever *do* anything. I mean, how can we create an extraordinary life if there's no trying at all? You can't be telling me that it's wrong to set goals and make plans and work hard?"

"Good point. It's all a balance, isn't it? All those things you mentioned flow from the head, and that's fine. Now, for you, it's time to bring in the heart. Stop trying to control your life and the ways of nature. You don't know what's best for you. You really don't."

"I guess my intelligence can't possibly be more powerful than the intelligence that runs the world," I recognized.

"Brilliant insight, Jack. So open yourself up more. There's a much larger world out there than you know. Live in the curiosity. Live in the awe. Live in the wonder."

I loved the sound of that.

"Begin to grow more aware and conscious," Moe continued. "Look for clues, spot the patterns, and connect the dots. Detect the synchronicity and the serendipity, and know that these beautiful coincidences are nothing more than your best life coming to get you. You can practice awareness by simply paying more attention to what's happening around you. Become more mindful of the dance of life. As you walk to work, for instance, rather than getting caught up in your internal dialogue, train your mind to detect what's going on in the outside world. Notice the color of the sky and the shapes of the clouds. Observe the leaves falling from the trees and way the sun feels as it warms your face. Feel the soles of your feet meet with Mother Earth. I even suggest you begin to pay attention to the way your heart beats. By practicing being more mindful, you'll get out of your head and move into your heart. You'll experience more living in your days. And you'll have a lot more fun. An even more powerful way to get out of your head and into your heart and body is to simply . . . get out of your head and into your body."

"Huh?" I said, confused.

"One of the most effective ways to get out of your head and away from all of that mental chatter that prevents us from living in the present moment is to spend more time in your body."

"How do I do this?"

"Pay attention to the sensations of your body," came the reply. "On those days that your mind is running at a frenetic place, consciously ask yourself, 'How do I feel?' 'What sensations are going on in my body right now?' 'Is there a tightness in my chest or a twitch in my foot or a pain in my heart?' This powerful little technique will immediately pull you out of your mind and draw you into your heart. And when you live in your heart more, you'll notice that you enjoy the journey of life more."

"The struggling ends," I added.

"It really does. You really don't have to figure it all out, Jack. That's all your fears at play. Life is a great mystery novel that contains the story of your life. What fun would it be if you knew how it all unfolded and how it ended before you got to the final chapter? What would happen if someone told you how a hot new movie ended before you even went to see it?"

"I wouldn't be amused—the fun would be gone."

"Right. As you say, 'The universe is a friendly place,' and no matter what happens, it's happening for the best. Your destiny will unfold as it's meant to unfold. In the meantime, enjoy the present. Live it fully. Live it authentically. Live it joyfully. Live it from the core of your heart. Life will take care of itself."

"But enough teaching for another day. Let's go surfing!"

And with that, Moe Jackson, the millionaire-advertising-genius-turned-hippie-surfer jumped up, grabbed his trusted surfboard, and headed out to sea.

———— ✦ ————

9 GROWTH ON A BEACH

*"The process of life should be the birth of a soul.
This is the highest alchemy, and this justifies our
presence on earth. This is our calling and our virtue."*

— Henri Frédéric Amiel

———— ✦ ————

The first two weeks with Moe were some of the most amazing days of my life. We'd get up early, have a fresh fruit breakfast together, and then spend the next few hours walking along the beach while he shared his wisdom on opening the heart and feeling love for life. I grew enormously fond of this wonderful man who taught me the ways of the heart and the value of being more playful, spontaneous, and spirited. I admired what he'd done—leaving the material world to chase his heartsong. And I respected the person he'd grown into. Like Father Mike before him, Moe was gentle, kind, and full of love.

"One of the best ways I've found to live out of your heart more is to shift from condemnation to compassion," Moe began telling me one morning as he tanned himself on the beach. "The very act of building some mindfulness around being a more loving person will open up your heart beautifully. Pay more attention to the way you treat other people. Spend more time focusing on their strengths rather than noting their weaknesses. Remember that on your deathbed, you'll never regret having been the most loving person you knew or having been someone who trusted people and showered them with unconditional love. Actually, at the end of your life, you just might find that that was the best, most fulfilling thing you ever did. By growing more deliberate and intentional in terms of the amount of love and kindness you deliver to other people, you'll strengthen *your* heart. It seems like an obvious technique to build up your heart muscles, yet it's easily overlooked."

"But isn't being more mindful living in the head once again?" I asked as I sliced a watermelon on a wooden bench that sat next to Moe's garden.

"Fair question. Yes and no. Being mindful does happen in the head, but it serves to help you create a bridge to the heart."

"Okay. Then how can I build some mindfulness around being a more loving person?"

"Well, one of the things that helps me is to meditate on being the loving person I want to be."

"I've been hearing a lot about meditation these days. What's it all about?" I inquired.

"Meditation is nothing more that using your mind and its imagination to create a better inner life," Moe answered. "It's all about envisioning the way you'd like to be in certain circumstances. Meditation is glorified visualization—nothing more than mental concentration with a personal-development twist to it. But by doing it on a regular basis, you'll actually open up new pathways in your brain and soften up your heart. You'll also begin to access the love within you. You goal is to be more loving in the world, right?"

I nodded. "Right."

"Great. So when you get up in the morning—and I'd like you to try this over the next few days—find a serene place along our beach and sit in a comfortable position. Then close your eyes and start breathing deeply. To breathe properly is to live properly, and breathing slowly and deeply will calm you. It will move you out of your head and into your body, into your heart."

"So some of my mental chatter will leave?"

"Of course it will. Now please stay with me here, Jack. As you grow more and more relaxed, you'll grow more and more open to suggestion. This is when you can begin to rescript the way you behave in your life and create a template for being a more loving human being. It's almost as if, in this state, you become an architect creating your ideal drawing. And once that drawing is done on the canvas of your imagination, the external world can manifest it according to your personal design."

"Great way to put it, Moe. So if I meditate every day and paint these pictures of being more kind and caring in my mind, I'll translate it into my reality?"

"You can't help but do so—it's one of the most important laws of nature. Meditate on how you wish to treat the people in your life, Jack. Actually see yourself acting in a more compassionate way in the difficult situations that regularly present themselves to you. You can also do 'open heart' meditations, such as imagining your heart to be a flower, and then watching it open up and pour its love out into the universe."

"Neat."

"And doing this kind of exercise on a daily basis will help you shift from condemning and finding fault with the people close to you to seeing them in their light, with compassion and authentic love. You'll be able to see their innocence, and love them for who they truly are. Another important way to open up the heart is to be more helpful. This strategy also sounds like common sense, but common sense is anything but common these days," Moe remarked as he adjusted his sunglasses.

"I agree. I once heard a speaker say that the easiest things to do are also the things that are easiest *not* to do."

"True enough. You can make some quantum leaps in your heart work by getting good at selflessly serving. The best way to reduce your personal suffering is to reduce the suffering of others, you know. The more you genuinely help other people, the more your heart will begin to beat to a new rhythm. The more you give to others with the sincere intention of lifting their lives to a higher level, the more the world will reward you by uplifting you. It's not hard stuff—it just takes commitment and an understanding of how it all works. And I should emphasize that giving with the expectation of a reward is not really giving. Antoine de Saint-Exupéry put it perfectly when he wrote: 'Real love begins where nothing is expected in return.' Just think about it, Jack—when you open your heart to another human being and genuinely help them, how does that make you feel?"

"It makes me feel great," I replied as I reflected on those rare occasions of the past where I'd been more interested in the welfare of another than in my own personal gain.

"Right. Every time you do something good for another person—and this point is really important—you not only improve their lives, you also improve your own self-worth. The more you serve other people, the better you'll feel about yourself at a root level. Your self-esteem will rise and you'll feel better about yourself as a human being. And at a deep level within, something will begin to shift and grow. You know what that is?"

"No?"

"It's your self-respect, the amount of love you have for

yourself." Moe took a sip of water from his canteen and offered it to me. "Want some?"

"No, thanks. I'm fine for now."

"What's mine is yours, Jack."

I knew he meant it.

"I'll bet you think I never leave this beach, right?" Moe asked, shifting gears in the conversation.

"I wondered about that. But it's a pretty stunning place— I wouldn't blame you if you never left."

"Well, let me share something with you. Every Friday morning, my friend Samantha drops by in her beat-up old pickup truck, and we head into town. We spend the rest of the morning cooking at the local shelter for the homeless and the displaced. That's one the most important activities in my life—it adds deep meaning to me and makes me feel like I'm a contributing member of society. 'Happiness comes from devoting your life to helping others'—I'd read that concept in books before, but as I started living it, I realized just how true it is. I personally believe that service and acts of kindness to others is the rent we pay for tenancy on this planet. Please remember that the hand that gives is the hand that gathers, and giving begins the receiving process."

"So when I return home, I could pay more attention to helping others," I told him. "I could be more of a friend to my friends and really think about being there for them when they need me most. I could make some time every week to volunteer or do some form of community service. I could really support the people I care about in achieving their dreams and living their highest truth in life, rather than worrying so much about what's in it for me. Come to think of it, I could practice being more giving by simply performing acts of kindness and love with strangers on the street. It would be fun to pay the toll for the person behind me on the bridge I go over on the way to work each day. It would be so great to buy a coffee for someone at the café I frequent. It would be amazing to share a little more of myself with the people around me—I could let people go in front of me in traffic jams and smile more as I go about my days. I really feel the value of this, Moe."

"Those are excellent ideas—especially supporting the dreams of others and the performance of good deeds to strangers. Doing good things for people each day sounds like such a simple strategy, yet it's one of those things that we all forget to do. I've always believed that a great life is measured not by decades but by deeds. But I should say that by far, the best way I've grown into a place where I can show boundless love for others is by growing into a place where I show boundless love for myself. Jack, I promise that your life will shift to a whole new plane once you practice the art of self-loving."

"I really want to love myself more," I said. "So you're saying that I can't give love to another if I don't feel true love for myself?"

He nodded. "Yes. Self-love is the fuel that drives personal change and helps you grow into a more loving person for others."

"I've been thinking a lot about self-love over the past few days, Moe. I thought I loved myself, but the deeper I go, the more I realize that there are so many parts of myself that I've denied. I think I have a lot of anger within me over some of the things that have happened to me over the course of my life. And I'm just becoming aware of it and how it seeps into every interaction I have with others, as well as the way I live with myself."

"Well, you need to work through that. Most of us have a ton of unfelt anger that we project out into the world, which colors everything we do and who we are as people. It even attracts people into our lives who exhibit their own anger as they relate to us. So you need to clear the anger that's hardened your heart; then you need to move through the sadness that will follow. Next you'll need to work through the fear and regret that are the next layers covering your heart. And only then can you find the forgiveness required to move on with your life. You know that forgiveness is something you do for yourself, don't you?"

"Really?"

"Yes. All of your past hurts that remain to be forgiven ride on your back, dragging you down as you try to advance through your life. When you do the inner work involved to work through those hurts by feeling your anger and then experiencing your sadness en route to moving into forgiveness, you'll get those monkeys off your back—once and for all. A huge weight is released, a new lightness enters your world, and then you can move forward and bring the light you are to the world. Remember, you can't get to second base with one foot on first, and staying stuck in your past wounds is nothing more than staying stuck on first base. Keep going deeper and deeper, Jack, and release more of your past. Soon you'll get to second base, then to third. A day will eventually come when you reach home."

"And the journey of life is really a journey back home," I said. "Father Mike taught me that one."

"Once again, Father Mike's right. I also love what Mark Twain said: 'Forgiveness is the fragrance the violet sheds on the heel that crushed it,'" Moe said with a grin.

"Oh, that's a great one!" I replied enthusiastically.

"You see, Jack, forgiveness isn't about condoning what someone did to you in the past—it's about accepting it and realizing that they only hurt you because they were in some form of fear. As I do my own inner work around accepting some of the things that have given me pain in my life, I often refer to the

Serenity Prayer, which says: 'God grant me the serenity to accept the things I cannot change, courage to change the things I can, and wisdom to know the difference.'"

"That's a pretty evolved way to live, Moe—seeing someone who has hurt you as being in a state of fear."

"But I feel it's true. In life, you're either in a state of love—"

"Or in a state of fear," I interrupted.

"Yes, how'd you know that? Father Mike again?"

"Father Mike again," I smiled.

"Well, he knows what he's talking about. If you're not acting out of love for another person—and it could be anyone from your mother to a stranger—you're acting out of fear. So someone who hurts you does so because they're in some fear at a deep level."

"I think an example would help me here, Moe. This is a tricky concept, and I'm finding it hard to wrap my head around it," I admitted, as I joined him on the sand to sunbathe.

"No sweat. Let's say that you run a business and one of your employees rips you off for a lot of money."

"That would be difficult to forgive."

"But he's done so out of fear, so why wouldn't you forgive him?"

"How has he acted out of fear? The guy took my money!"

"A person is either acting out of love or he's acting from fear, right?" Moe asked pointedly. "Fear doesn't have to mean fear of personal safety. That's just one kind of fear. There are many other forms that control us at deep levels. We might have a fear of being taken advantage of. We might have a fear of looking stupid. We might have a fear of being abandoned. We might have a fear of being unsupported. We might have a fear of being betrayed."

"So what fear might have been motivating this thief from

your example?" I inquired, intrigued by the philosophy I was hearing.

"It could have been a fear of scarcity—maybe he has no awareness of how incredibly abundant our world truly is and how its riches flow into life when one lets go of the fear that there's not enough. Maybe he has a deep-rooted belief that he's unable to live a prosperous life if he works hard and treats people well—so he stole your money. Or he might have a fear of not being competent as a human being and as your employee—so he's afraid of being fired. He needs money to feed his family, so he steals *your* money. His actions are clearly wrong, and his behavior is not to be condoned, but he's in fear. He is, and again this is happening at a deep psychological level, frightened. Do you punish a frightened child?"

"No, I guess not."

"Well, what would you do?" asked Moe.

"I'd give the child love—I'd support her, console her, and help her."

"Exactly. And that's what you need to do the man who steals your money. You forgive him, help him, and show him love."

"I show him love?" I asked in disbelief.

"Yes, ideally you would. And if you could, you'd be operating at such an extraordinarily high level of enlightenment and personal power that your life would be nothing but joy. In this state, the most amazing treasures would be attracted to you as you moved through your days. In the case of our thief, at the very least, you'd need to forgive him if you wanted to move forward in your life. It would be important to work through how he hurt you, accept that the event happened, and then release it from your system. To truly move forward, you'd have to let it go and understand that this occurrence carried with it some corresponding gift. There was an opportunity and a lesson in the pain you endured—get the lesson and move on."

"Life's a growth school, right?"

"It really is," replied Moe.

"I need to do more of this letting go you speak of because I seem to replay the things people have done to me in the past over and over—it's like an obsession. It tires me out and drains my energy. Sometimes I just want to go to sleep and forget about all the things I'm worrying about," I offered with honesty.

"I have a sense that you really don't know how blessed you are, Jack. I suggest that you get some perspective on all the good that's in your life. Makes me think of that old proverb that says: 'I wept because I had no shoes on my feet until I saw the man without any feet.'"

Those words struck my heart. I felt emotion welling up within me.

"Our lives can change when we become more aware of all the positives we live with," Moe continued, "when we start living with a greater sense of perspective and a greater appreciation of the truth. So few of us really know the truth about our lives—we get caught up in our own stories. Like we were just discussing, we get caught up in things that happened to us a year ago or two years ago or ten years ago. Jack, I also used to spend entire days worrying about things people did to me many years before. I'd make the slights bigger than they were. I'd think about getting revenge and how I could make people pay for what they did to me. It was a really small way to conduct a life, I'll tell you that much."

"I really am very much like you used to be. I do the same thing, but I'm going to stop."

"Confucius once said: 'Before you set out to seek revenge, it is best to dig two graves,'" Moe laughed.

"Brilliant point, Moe. God, we take ourselves seriously!

We're all so self-absorbed that we think we're at the center of the universe. We fool ourselves into believing that our troubles are the biggest and only troubles in the world. But we're not as important as we think we are, are we? Stephen Hawking, the great physicist, is reported to have said that we're on a minor planet of a very average star located within the outer limits of one of a hundred thousand million galaxies. Given this, I really see how our problems and frustrations aren't so big. We walk this planet for a very short time, and yet we're so serious about it all."

"Yes, we do," Moe agreed. "We all need to develop a greater appreciation for the gifts in our lives. And by appreciating what's good in our lives, those good things will grow."

"How so?"

"Think in terms of economics: When something appreciates in value, let's say your house, what happens to it?"

"Well, to say something appreciates means that it goes up in price. It becomes worth more."

"Okay. The same holds true for things you appreciate in your life: If you appreciate the sunrise, it will become a more valuable part of your life, and you'll attach more worth to it. If you appreciate your friends, their friendship will go up in value, and it will be worth more to you. If you appreciate your good health, it will become more valuable in your life, and you'll see it as being more important."

"Wow, that's a very intelligent way of looking at things," I remarked energetically.

"I guess the real point is this: Living in a state of constant and never-ending gratitude will make the experience of life far more valuable and worthwhile. The way you see the world will change— you'll enjoy life's little pleasures so much more and savor the tiny blessings each day delivers. You *must* practice gratitude more often. And doing so is yet another way to open up your heart and love your life. Practicing gratitude daily is nothing more than practicing love daily."

"So how can I practice gratitude?" I asked.

"One of the things I do each day is bless my food. Before each meal, I give silent and sincere thanks for the meal I'm about to enjoy: I thank the farmers who grew the produce, the fisherman who caught the fish, and the sellers at the market for making it all available. And I give thanks to the world for granting me the privilege of having food on my table in a world where millions upon millions of people don't have enough to eat. This is a simple little technique, but it will create profound shifts in you. Trust me on this one."

"Sounds powerful. I guess by appreciating your food, you increase its value in your life, and you begin to stop taking it for granted, right?"

"Right. And in performing this ritual, my heart opens up and I see the world as a more beautiful, giving place. Like I said earlier, doing this will help you begin to gain perspective on how fortunate you really are."

"Good point," I replied. "In this part of the world, we really don't realize how much we have. We don't count our blessings."

"Yup. I love writing blessing lists. They keep me centered on all the good I have in life."

"What's a blessing list?"

"It's simply a recording of all of the things, no matter how small, that I love about my life. I write down the fact that I live on this beach. I write down the fact that I'm in wonderful health. I write down the fact I'm a great dancer. I note the fact that I get to sleep under the stars every night. And, as I say, I remember that I'm blessed to have food in my belly every day. I could go on and on. The point is simply this: Each and every one of us has a ton of things to be grateful for, yet most of us focus on lack rather than abundance. And the funny thing is, the more you focus on what's good about your life, the more good you'll seem to attract."

"Any other practices I could do to create an attitude of gratitude?" I wondered.

"I strongly suggest that you develop a daily prayer. This has nothing to do with being religious—that's your personal business. The prayer I'm speaking of has everything to do with being thankful. Create a short, emotionally charged prayer that expresses your heartfelt appreciation for all you have. Recite this prayer first thing in the morning and last thing at night. Once again, the results you see will be spectacular."

Moe studied me for a moment. "Jack, these tools I'm giving you might seem a bit odd. But the main thing is they work. Oh, there are two more ways to really build your personal gratitude muscles. One is to send love letters."

"But I'm not in love with anyone."

"You don't have to be. These love letters are of a different sort—they're not about romantic love, they're about human love. Here's an example. Let's say that you go out to dinner and the meal is exquisite. The next morning, I recommend that you send a 'love letter' to the chef expressing how much you loved his meal and commending him on his exceptional talents. He'd feel so happy."

"And I'd feel great."

"Right. This would increase your self-worth, you'd feel better about yourself, and you'd feel more blessed in your life. If you take your car to get serviced, and the person who cares for you does a masterful job, send a 'love letter' to his boss telling her that you loved the service and appreciate the kindness. Constantly be on the lookout for people you can send such letters to. In fact, I recommend that when you return home you go out and buy a package of 100, or even 200, cards. I'm always keeping my eyes open for those with great quotes or inspirational messages on them. When I find ones that I like, I buy them in bulk. Then, whenever someone does something nice for me, they get my love letter."

"But you hardly ever leave this beach, Moe."

"Well, for the past few weeks, I've been here with you—because I have a mission to help you, as I promised Cal I would. But I generally make it into town every few days. And when I do, I hunt for opportunities to express my gratitude."

"You mentioned that there was a second thing to do."

"Right. The final tool to show gratitude is to give every person you meet a gift."

"That could get expensive," I observed earnestly.

"I don't mean a formal gift," Moe said. "It could be as simple as giving someone you meet a true smile. It might mean giving someone a hug or a sincere compliment in a world where we've forgotten the importance of genuine praise. You could bring someone a single, fresh flower from your garden or a hot muffin you just baked. Even listening to someone with complete attention and a wide-open heart is a gift that will touch people in places you can't imagine."

Moe moved closer to me. He began to stare deeply into my eyes, with a gentle smile on his face. He didn't say a word—he just kept on looking into my eyes with total concentration.

After a few moments, something incredible happened. I felt as if something in my chest opened up. I also felt the same sense of comfort and security I used to feel as a little boy when my mother would hug me before I'd go to sleep.

"What are you doing to me?" I asked Moe. "I'm having these amazing feelings."

"I'm doing what I always try to do when I'm in the presence of another human being, Jack. I'm sending you love. My heart is wide open, and I'm just appreciating all that you are as a person. My heart is speaking to your heart, and you're feeling that. When we interact with others, there's a lot more going on than we're consciously aware of."

"It's extraordinary to feel all the love you're sending me," I replied.

"I know," remarked Moe. "This is my greatest gift to you."

Moe then reached over and gave me a big hug. I noticed that his eyes were brimming with tears. "You're a good man, Jack," he said. "I pray that you put all you're learning and growing to good use. Our world so desperately needs people who are more caring, understanding, and loving. You can be a leader to so many if you become a model of these qualities in your own life—I just know it. Trust in the fact that the more love you give to others, the more love you'll feel for yourself. And trust that the more you open up your heart, the more your best life will reveal itself to you."

Moe began walking toward the water. He then dipped one foot in before moving in deeper. Soon he was swimming gracefully and staring out at the horizon. I could hear him laughing and singing while he splashed away. As I watched this wise teacher enjoying the gift of the moment, something deep within me began to change . . . and for some reason, I began to cry.

10 SURFING AND SELF-LOVE

"It is only when we forget all our learning that we begin to know."

— Henry David Thoreau

———— ✦ ————

O ver the next week, I went deeper into my heart than ever before. I'd been integrating not only Moe's lessons but Father Mike's wisdom as well for some time now, and the changes that were occurring in my life were truly surprising. The philosophies I'd been learning actually worked, even though some of them seemed a bit mystical. I could feel myself transforming at a pace quicker than I ever could have imagined. I really was beginning to connect to a higher version of myself and see the world through a new set of eyes, as Father Mike had encouraged me to do. Not only that, but I was feeling happier than ever before, and a deep sense of inner peace had started to form within me. Love was something I really hadn't felt before, at least not like this. Now I was experiencing it—not in relation to another person, although I knew that was coming, but in relation to myself.

"You're getting to be a pretty good surfer there, Jack," Moe told me on the first day of our final week together. He'd been helping me learn the sport he loved so much, and now he beamed with pride. "You're a natural, you know."

"It's become a passion of mine—one of those things that makes my heart sing. I feel like a kid again when I'm surfing with you. It's so outrageously fun. Thanks so much for turning me on to it," I told him.

"You're welcome. Before we hit the waves today, I want to talk a little more about self-love. I've shared lots of knowledge with you over the past three weeks, and it's pretty obvious that things are really shifting for you."

"What's happening for me is pretty miraculous, Moe. I'm really grateful to you."

"No sweat. That's what I'm here for. What's the purpose of living if you can't help others, right?"

"Right."

"Anyway, you're doing great. You can promote self-loving," Moe continued, "by wisely using the language you choose to describe yourself with. The vocabulary of words we use is far more important than many of us realize. If you don't speak kindly in your self-talk and select loving words for your inner dialogue, than you can't be kind to others. The more love you give yourself, the more you'll have available for others—you've learned that by now. You can't give away something that you don't have, can you?"

I shook my head. "No."

"So it's key to keep remembering that you own the love within yourself. Then, and only then, will you be in a position to give authentically to all around you. What I'm saying is: Be good to yourself. Be *really* good to yourself. Treat yourself as you would your greatest hero. And a way to begin is by speaking well to yourself. The words we use hold tremendous power, Jack.

There's a specific energy attached to each word we use."

"There is?"

"Yes. Everything in this world is nothing more than energy. Did you study physics in college by any chance?"

"As a matter of fact, I did. I took a few science courses because I thought about going to medical school at one time."

"Great. So let me ask you: Is this surfboard here really a surfboard?"

I felt confused. "Well, yes . . . isn't it?"

"Remember, go back to the laws of physics. All things that appear material to the naked eye are really—"

"Energy!" I interjected.

"Correct. This surfboard is nothing more than subatomic particles moving at an incredibly fast rate of speed. And those subatomic particles, as any good physicist will tell you, are nothing more than energy. To the human eye, your surfboard appears as a solid object. But it's not—that's the illusion of life."

"So everything in the world is nothing more than energy," I mused. "I know that's true, and yet it's so easy to forget this fact. You're right. We do buy into the illusion that material objects are what they initially appear to be."

"Yes," Moe replied.

"And the words we choose to use are nothing more than energy as well?"

"For sure. Just as the thoughts we think are nothing more than bundles of energy that we send out into the world, the words we speak are messengers."

"What exactly do you mean?"

"I don't want to get too technical here, but we live in what physicists have called a *holographic universe*, which means that what we send out comes back in kind. If we think thoughts of scarcity, for example, we'll attract greater scarcity into our lives because those thoughts are nothing more than energy, and like attracts like. If we think thoughts of fear, fearful situations will prevail. That's why the great leader Mahatma Gandhi said: 'I will not let anyone walk through my mind with their dirty feet.'"

"Can you explain this a little more?" I asked, truly fascinated by this point.

"Okay. A thought about scarcity, such as *I never have enough money, and it's hard to become wealthy* has a certain energy and rate at which the particles that form this thought vibrate at."

"Makes sense."

"And we know from physics that things that vibrate at the same rate are drawn to one another."

"Okay."

"So the thoughts you think are actually like magnets, attracting into your life people and events that harmonize with them."

"Are you serious?" I asked, stunned by this revelation.

"Yes, I am. It's incredible, isn't it? Our thinking actually sets up a self-fulfilling prophecy. If we think the world is a scarce place, then that's the reality we'll end up creating. If we think that we're unlovable and no one would want to be with us if they truly discovered who we are, then we'll never find that soulmate we've been longing for. If we believe that life is hard, then the world will send us a hard life."

"Truly remarkable. So every time I think about what's not working in my life, I'm actually making things worse."

"Yes."

"And every moment I focus on what I don't like about my life, I'm actually blocking what I *do* want from entering."

"Correct. Can you see that our thoughts really do form our world? What you focus on in your life will grow, what you think about will expand, and what you dwell on will determine your destiny. This is far more than a bunch of motivational jargon.

These statements are based on the laws of nature and scientific fact."

"Isn't this just positive thinking? I thought you told me that positive thinking was basically unhealthy—now you're saying it isn't."

"Well, I don't think it's as black-and-white as you're saying, Jack. There's so much more involved."

"Like what?"

"Like feelings, for example. Positive thinking really isn't healthy if it means that rather than seeing how you might feel in a challenging situation you deny it and 'think happy thoughts,'" Moe replied, echoing what Father Mike had taught me during the month I'd spent in Rome.

He went on. "It's essential to our emotional health that we notice and experience our feelings. Doing so is part of accepting and loving all of ourselves; it also prevents the feelings from adding to the baggage that we all carry along with us through life. In addition, our feelings open doorways into greater awareness and offer up remarkable insights, and feeling through them keeps us clear. But once you've completed a feeling to its endpoint, which every feeling has, then there's certainly nothing wrong with looking for the good in the circumstance. Actually, that's the only smart thing to do."

"Why?"

"First, because in every situation, there's always some good—everything that happens to us represents an opportunity to grow and evolve into our best selves. Second, because this is the only way to live a peaceful and happy life. And third, because, as I'm telling you, our thoughts are like magnets, attracting into our life people and instances that harmonize with them. Keep focusing on the negative and that's what your life will be. Train yourself to concentrate on the good in any situation—and there always is if you look hard enough for it—and that's what you'll see more of in your reality."

"Our thoughts form our world. Very cool."

"And I should also mention that the *pictures* you create within your inner world cannot help but manifest themselves in your outer world. I call this process *out-picturing*. The internal will always become your external because all things are created twice: first in your mind and then in reality. Any picture that you imagine, if focused on daily for an extended period of time, cannot help but appear in your outer world. Envision yourself as being a kind, loving, and confident human being, and that's exactly what you'll grow into. Imagine yourself as happy, playful, and rich with a childlike heart, and that's what you'll eventually be. It's a beautiful tool that I know will be of immense value to you on this path you're on."

"Now, Moe, before you got into this amazing discussion about the world being nothing more than energy and the laws of physics and the holographic universe, you were saying that the words we use have great power. I have a much better sense of why this is so now, but could your please clarify this point?"

"Sure. Just as our thoughts shape our worlds, so do our words. It's essential that you become very careful about the words you speak—not only to others but to yourself. If you use words that are positive and full of power, you'll become positive and more powerful. You'll also influence people in ways more profound than you ever could have imagined."

Moe then began walking along the beach. It was yet another gorgeous day, and the sunlight danced along the water, creating a magical effect.

"C'mon! What are you waiting for?" he asked, leaving his surfboard in the sand and heading toward his tiny hut. "There's something I'd like to show you."

We walked in silence, but Moe had a smile on his face as he gracefully made his way along the shore, stepping in and out of the water as he approached his destination. I sensed a deep joy in this "simple" man. He owned so little, yet he had so much.

——— ✦ ———

When we arrived at Moe's hut, he ducked inside for a moment. "Hang on for a moment, Jack. You're going to love this," he remarked playfully.

Within a few seconds he reappeared, holding something odd in his hands. It was a surfboard with both ends chopped off.

"This used to be my favorite surfboard," he said. "Now it's my wordboard."

"What's a wordboard?" I asked with great curiosity.

"Here, look at this," he replied as he flipped the board over to reveal a series of hand-carved words in the wood. "As I've said, words have power. Use the right words and your life will change. You'll grow in power, your confidence will soar, and you'll discover a degree of self-love that you never knew you had." He pointed to the board. "I read these words, slowly and aloud, every night before I go to sleep. This nightly practice opens my heart and connects me to my internal brilliance. Here, Jack. Read them."

I looked at the words and spoke each one out loud, slowly and confidently: "Harmony. Peace. Kindness. Happiness. Joy. Wisdom. Vitality. Truth. Fun. Compassion. Abundance. Forgiveness. Balance. Courage."

"Now repeat the last and most important one," Moe said.

"Love," I stated,

"Keep doing this practice on a regular basis. It really will change you. You'll feel more compassion for yourself and others.

You'll elevate your consciousness. And you'll continue to open up your heart."

"This is a very innovative technique, Moe. I like it a lot. Who taught it to you?"

"You know, Jack, the more I get to know myself, the more I realize that everything I really need to know to create an extraordinary life lives in here," he said, pointing directly to his heart. "Of course, as I told you, it's a balance. The mind can offer you wonderful insights that empower you and connect the dots along the path of your life—but I have to say that it really doesn't compare to the intelligence and wisdom that lives in your heart. This technique I just shared with you didn't come from a book. It came to me one day as I did a meditation I'd been using to keep opening my heart. You know, the deeper I get in there and the more love I feel for myself—and the world—the more the universe seems to bless me with wisdom, truth, and amazing ideas for an extraordinary life. I can't explain it—that's just the way it is for me."

"I guess at times I'm afraid to trust my heart completely," I confided. "I've spent so much of my life trusting what my head tells me is the right way to think, feel, and act."

"And has that brought you the kind of life you've always wanted, Jack? Has that strategy really delivered on its promise?"

"No," I admitted.

"So maybe it's time to put a lot more faith in your heart. Just maybe, the work you're doing to open up your heart is exactly what you need to get to the next stage of your path."

"Well, I know it is," I replied. "I guess it's just my fear. I don't want to get hurt, and I don't want to mess up my life any more than it has been. I guess what I'm really afraid of is making any more mistakes."

Moe placed his hand on my shoulder to comfort me.

"A mistake is only a mistake if you repeat it," he said. "The first time, it's nothing more than a beautiful lesson—you know that. Be gentle with yourself. You're doing great. This is big stuff you're walking into. Just make sure that the mistakes of your past are nothing but wonderful gifts that came to you to get you to where you are now. Each one of the problems that challenged you in the past was designed by the universe to raise you to your next level of awareness. Setbacks, struggles, and suffering all serve to open us up—they're sent to us to improve us. Pain, for example, is a gift."

I wasn't sure I heard him correctly. "Pain is a gift?"

"Of course it is. It deepens us and introduces us to who we truly are. The ancient seers believed that those who suffered the most in life were the most blessed."

"I can't imagine why."

"Because sadness stretches us," Moe replied as he peeled an orange.

"It does?"

"Yes—it opens us to the wonder of life that we otherwise would have missed. A life without setbacks is a shallow life. To fully experience your life, you must experience the highs as well as the lows—then you'll know what being alive is really about. Pain isn't such a bad thing, you know. Actually, I believe that pain comes to us to raise our lives to the next level."

"I never thought of it that way."

"And I believe that the people who endure more pain and suffering are meant for greater things on the planet. The more pain in one's life, the more your eyes open up to the truth. You see, Jack, pain strengthens. Pain leads to possibility. Pain deepens you and reveals you to yourself. Pain causes growth in human beings. I love the words of Thomas Carlyle, who said: 'Adversity is the diamond dust Heaven polishes its jewels with.'

You're a jewel, Jack. Every one of us on the planet today is a jewel, here for a magnificent purpose. I wish more people understood this truth."

"I do, too," I replied wistfully.

"Everything that happens to us is all part of the grand design and grist for the mill—it adds color, texture, and depth to our lives. Easy lives really are shallow lives. And so, we shouldn't fear adversity, we should embrace it. As Aristotle said: 'The beauty of the soul shines out when a man bears with composure one heavy mischance after another, not because he does not feel them but because he is a man of high and heroic temper.'"

Moe grew quiet and looked out over the ocean. "Okay, back to my advice on being self-loving. Another great way to be really good to yourself is to ensure that there are a lot of self-care activities in your life."

"Okay . . . what are 'self-care' activities all about, Moe?"

"These are things you do to show you how much you love yourself. I'm speaking of activities such as getting a massage on a regular basis or carving out some time every week to watch the stars twinkle. I'm speaking of things like feeding yourself excellent food because you respect the temple that's your body. And I'm referring to reading only the best books and listening to lovely music that sends your spirit soaring. Self-care—it's one of the great keys to self-love."

Moe took a few pieces of his orange and handed the rest to me. "Here, this is for you. I'd like to share five self-care practices that I use in my own life to keep me balanced, relaxed, and playful. May I?"

"Of course."

"First, shift from complexity to simplicity."

"Please elaborate," I requested.

"We live in a complex world, and we each take on complex

lives. The more we shift from being to doing, the more our lives take on a complexity that creates disorder, chaos, and stress. Always be moving toward simplicity—keep asking yourself, 'How can I make my life simpler?' That's an extremely powerful question to live your life with. Be wary of anything that comes into your life and makes it more complicated—from a difficult relationship to an extra newspaper subscription. One of the organizing principles that any great life is built around is this one: 'Simplify, simplify, simplify.' My life is so very simple, Jack. And as a result, it's so very beautiful. It's nice and lean—just the way I like it. No cell phones. No junk mail. No television. *Simple.*"

"Just the sound of that brings a feeling of ease to me," I remarked.

"When I was working in the advertising world, I literally had every minute of my life scheduled. I planned out my meeting times and my times for getting work projects done. I planned when I took breaks and when I made phone calls. I planned the exact hours I worked out with my personal trainer and the time when I connected with my girlfriend. I even scheduled when I slept and ate into an hour-by-hour plan."

"Sounds extremely complex, even by my standards."

"*Extreme* is the right word, sport. There was no time for free flow."

"What's that?"

"Free flow is a state of living where you have present-moment awareness. Every cell within you is engaged in the moment you're living. Hey, there's nothing wrong with planning your weeks, don't get me wrong—but don't let your plan own you. It's all about a balance, isn't it?"

"Like all of life."

"Right. So leave space—and lot's of it—to enjoy the precious moments of your life. Make time to enjoy the simple pleasures of the world, for they last a lot longer than the expensive ones. Don't be so busy chasing the big pleasures that you miss out on the little ones. Don't be so busy striving that you miss out on living. You know, deep down inside, I believe that most of us aren't really afraid of death."

This surprised me. "Really?"

"Yes. I believe that most of us are more afraid of not having truly lived."

"That makes sense," I replied reflectively.

Moe continued with his discourse on methods to renew and deepen ourselves. "The second self-care practice I encourage you to integrate into your life is the daily practice of journaling. Your life is worth living, isn't it?"

"Of course it is. I'm more confident about that now than I've ever been."

"Great. And since your life's worth living, it's worth recording. Every morning before I go surfing, I take some time to do my 'daily pages,' as I call them. I write about the tale of my life and the way it's unfolding. I write about my longings that remain unfulfilled and celebrate the victories that I've enjoyed. I write about what makes me happy and what makes me sad. I write about my pain and articulate the lessons I've learned from what wounded me in the past. There's something magical about pouring my heart out onto a crisp, white page every morning. It's almost as if I get to recreate my life every single day, and pour my vision of my ideal life out onto the canvas of reality every time the sun comes up. It's pretty incredible to know that every new day brings with it the opportunity to begin a whole new life."

"Do you truly believe that, Moe?"

"Yes, I do. It doesn't take a month or a year or a decade to change your life—it happens in an instant. It happens the moment you make a fundamental commitment from the deepest place within you that you'll no longer stand for mediocrity, and dedicate yourself to living the life you were destined to live."

"My best life."

"You got it."

"I guess you're right. That choice only takes a second to make."

"Yes," Moe agreed. "And if it's made from the core of your heart, something within you will shift. You'll no longer accept the way you've been living, and you'll automatically raise the bar of your life and set a series of new standards for yourself. Now while it only takes a minute to change your life, let's be real here. What takes the months, years, and decades is *maintaining* your best life. It's like working out at the gym: Once you condition your body to be its best form, you must maintain what you've created."

"Got it. So tell me more about journaling. I've been hearing a lot about this lately."

"It's an incredible way of exploring the deepest places of yourself and liberating your highest talents. For example, the very act of journaling allows me to release any worries that have cluttered my mind and arrive at profound insights that enrich my days. Journaling makes me a clearer thinker and gives me energy as I align my outer life with the one that lives within me. Journaling gives me a place to converse with myself, and in doing so, build greater self-awareness and create more self-knowledge. Journaling gives me a vehicle to capture all my ideas and record them for review at a later time. Just try it, Jack, and you'll begin to experience the benefits I'm talking about."

"So I should just write out my thoughts?"

"Well, I actually recommend that you begin this habit by simply spending some time each morning dumping out your consciousness onto the pages of your notebook. Let go of all the things that are creating fears and frustration in your life. Pour out everything that's chattering through your mind, and release it as a stream of consciousness. Record all the feelings that are coming up for you. Just start writing and keep writing, without lifting the pen from the page. And then stop when you're clear and feel liberated. This exercise will work wonders for your peace of mind, for your inner power, and for the best life that you're reclaiming."

"Very cool. Journaling really sounds amazing, Moe."

"It is. Just start writing down what's going on in your inner world every morning. Write about all of your irritations. And once the negative's been cleared out, articulate what's positive in your life and within your heart. I also suggest that you write about your big dreams and what I call your *Noble Goals.*"

"What are Noble Goals? I like the sound of that term."

"These are the greatest desires of your heart, the ones that will fuel your growth and shape you. Write about the person you are and whom you'd love to be. Just write freely—as the days go by, you'll go deeper and deeper. I also recommend that you answer, in writing, five questions every morning. These Morning Questions will take only a few minutes to answer, but they'll set you up for enormous success during your day."

"And what are these Morning Questions?"

"Number one is: 'How would I live out this day if I knew it was my last?' Two is: 'What do I have to be grateful for in my life?'"

"That one's good because it would help build my attitude of gratitude," I replied.

"Right. Three is: 'What one thing could I do today to help make my life extraordinary?' Four is: 'What can I do to make today incredibly fun?' And the fifth question is: 'How can I help someone today?'"

"And this little practice will be helpful to me?"

"Tremendously. Asking yourself these five questions, and then answering them every morning will connect you with your deepest wisdom. And that wisdom will then infuse every remaining minute of your day. You'll become better to those you love and work with, and even to people on the street. It's a very powerful practice."

"Moe, I hope you don't mind my saying this, but there seems to be a ton of things I need to be doing each day to create my best life. I'm feeling overwhelmed. And how would anyone have time to do all the things you're suggesting? I've got a career. I've got friends. I've got obligations."

"Good point, Jack. These are all ideas for you to consider. They've been tested and they work. *Experiment* with each one of them. Stay open to the possibilities they represent. And then, once you've explored each of them for a while, select the practices that work best for you and build them into your weeks as part of your winning formula for a great life so they're never neglected. And that's an extremely important point. In order to ensure that these practices get done on a regular basis, you must make them a part of your life. You'd never go to work without showering and shaving, would you?"

"Of course not."

"That's because those practices have been integrated into your routine. They've become conditioned into your life so that they get done automatically. You need to do the same for the practices that work best for you."

"Okay. That makes perfect sense," I replied.

Moe scratched his bare chest and then yawned. "Boy, I'm feeling laid-back today."

"Me, too."

"The third self-care practice I wish to share with you is that of a daily period of peace. You must make the time to have a silent retreat each day. You owe it to yourself."

"When I was a kid, Mom and I often spent time in the silence and stillness of the forest, just walking. I still remember how happy that made me feel," I reflected.

"A silent retreat is like that. It's nothing more than a little period of time you build into each and every one of your days to sit in stillness and quiet. Silence is nature's sweet restorer, opening up a space in our lives to connect with our best selves—it's a tonic that heals us and caresses our souls. Spending time in silence each day will strengthen you as a human being and deliver delightful results to your life. Withdraw into silence daily—you'll emerge a new man, with new confidence and higher ideas."

Moe passed his fingers through his thick blond hair. "We live in a world with too much noise and not enough quiet. It's so important to make time each day to be silent and still. As Blaise Pascal once wrote: 'I have discovered that all the unhappiness of men arises from one single fact, that they cannot stay quietly in their chamber.'"

"So well said," I remarked.

"The fourth self-care practice is communing with nature," Moe continued. "In doing so, we can direct our lives inward and connect with what's most important—we'll access a larger part of ourselves and connect with the universe. For instance, I find that being out there on the ocean, just me and my board, reminds me that I'm never alone. It frees me and opens me up. A life without regular periods in nature is a half-life as far as I'm concerned."

"I really used to love walking in the woods. I don't know

why I stopped that habit. I guess as life got busier, I gave up on these kinds of things. I never really appreciated how important they were to my well-being. Now I do."

"Good man, Jack. Nature will be a great friend to you, and you deserve a friend like that. Okay, the fifth self-care practice is nurturing your body. Your body is your temple—it's the place where your spirit lives, your home. To show leadership of your life and create the life I know you want, it's so important that you treat your body well. As you care for your body, so you'll care for your life."

"Really?"

"Sure. By taking care of your physical dimension, you'll make a wonderful investment in the quality and longevity of your life. What's the point of living a long time if you can't enjoy it by feeling good, strong, and healthy?"

"Makes sense. So what kinds of things do *you* do to nurture your body, Moe?"

"Well, one of the most important things I do is stay fit. I run along this beach every morning. I surf for much of the day. And in the evenings, I generally go for a long walk or do a little yoga up there on the top of that cliff," he said, pointing to a ridge that seemed to offer a striking view of the heavens above. "Those who don't make time for exercise must eventually make time for illness, you know."

That point really hit home for me.

Moe continued. "It never ceases to make me shake my head."

"What?" I asked.

"Well, we just don't get how important staying in good physical condition is for the creation of a beautiful life. When we're young, we sacrifice so much of our health in the pursuit of wealth. And then when we get old and wise, we change our tune—we become willing to sacrifice every bit of our wealth for even one day of good health. But by then it's too late. Don't let that happen to you, Jack. Please understand how central it is to be in superb condition. It's a great act of personal leadership, and its benefits will spill out into so many other areas of your life. You'll have more energy, your moods will be better, you'll be more creative, you'll have higher self-esteem, and you'll even find that your sleep improves."

"You're right, Moe. I completely agree with you. You have my word on this—I'll commit myself to getting into shape. I can really see how important this discipline is."

"I also make sure that I put only the best foods into my temple. Excellent nutrition is deeply important in the creation of an extraordinary life. Eating only the best foods available is a gift I give myself. It's a sign of self-respect. Eating low-grade foods is a terrible thing to do to yourself. My guess is that at a core level, anyone who does this on a regular basis needs to love themselves more."

"Makes sense."

"Sure. If you truly loved yourself, how could you eat anything other than great foods? Eating well really is a mark of self-respect, and it increases self-love."

"What kinds of food do you eat, Moe? Since I've been here, it's been mostly fruits and veggies."

"Simple stuff, such as live foods, suits me best. I love fresh fruit, as you know, and here on the island, I'm blessed to have that in abundant supply. I eat a ton of vegetables, and I'm a big fan of fish. Once in a while, I'll have other types of meat, but I try not to be extreme in my ways."

"All things in balance."

"Well said, Jack. That's the real key. Oh, another thing I do for my body is massage. I have a friend who swings by every week to give me a beautiful massage. It keeps my body supple, increases my circulation, and helps me stay at my best. Have you ever had a massage, my friend?"

"Actually, I haven't."

"Try to get one regularly. Actually, let me insist on it. You'll find that it will keep you very relaxed, highly energetic, and generally feeling great about yourself. It's another wonderful act of self-loving and treating yourself well. After all, life's too short to not be giving yourself lots of love."

———— ✦ ————

The final few days with Moe were spent talking, surfing, swimming, and playing.

I'd never met a man quite like Moe Jackson, and I sensed that I never would. Both he and Father Mike were true treasures: strong, wise, and powerful men with big hearts and large spirits.

On the day I was to leave Hawaii for New York, Moe strolled over to where I was lying on the beach, watching the clouds float across the clear blue sky.

"I'll miss you, Jack," he said.

"I'll miss you, too, Moe," I replied, feeling a deep sadness inside of me.

"Okay, amigo, it's time for you to go. Please keep in touch— I want to watch your star rise. I know you'll do great things and create a truly enchanting life for yourself. Hey, and if you ever feel the need to spend a week or two surfing, you know my 'palace' is yours, too," Moe said with a smile.

We hugged each other, and then I started walking toward the taxicab that was waiting for me at the other end of the beach.

"Moe," I said as I turned around, "thanks for being great."

"No sweat. Now, if you don't mind, me and my surfboard have a meeting with a wave."

And with that, this surfer with the heart of a child dashed into the ocean and chased his bliss.

THE
CEO

11 THE ONE WHO GIVES THE MOST WINS

"I don't know what your destiny will be, but one thing I do know: the only ones among you who will really be happy are those who have sought and found how to serve."

— Albert Schweitzer

"Just imagine that the purpose of life is your happiness only— then life becomes a cruel and senseless thing. You have to embrace what the wisdom of humanity, your intellect and your heart tell you: that the meaning of life is to serve the force that sent you into the world. Then life becomes a joy."

— Leo Tolstoy

—— ✦ ——

I'd always had a special place in my heart for New York City. It was one of those places that always stayed with me, no matter where I went. I loved the tasty pretzels that were sold on the streets, along with the thick, juicy hot dogs that probably shaved years off my life. I loved the majestic skyscrapers that gave the city its grand look of power. I loved the dazzling pace and electric energy, which inspired me to dream bigger dreams and take larger steps. I'd only been here a few times, but it felt great to be back.

The flight from Hawaii had been fun. There were just a few of us in the first-class cabin, and we all became friends as we flew across the Pacific. As I grew more comfortable with my seatmates, I began to share some of the lessons that I'd learned over the past two months. I told them about my time in Rome with Father Mike, and what he'd taught me about being authentic as a human being. I recited his theories on the way the world worked as a school for our growth, and how challenges were actually opportunities—if we had the wisdom to seize them. I discussed the concept of The Integrity Gap and how we betray ourselves when we're not true to ourselves. And I shared his stained glass window metaphor and how it applies to the filters through which each one of us see our world.

I also told my new friends about the extraordinary Moe Jackson, the eccentric surfer who I felt was a modern-day master. I revealed what he'd told me about living in the heart. I also shared his thoughts on standing in the mystery of our lives and releasing the control that the vast majority of us cling to in order to discover the true treasures that are meant for our lives. And I offered them his fascinating self-care practices for personal renewal and creating our best selves.

"You should write a book," the young woman next to me said sincerely. "I bet it would be a huge bestseller. The whole world is searching for wisdom like this—and it would be a better, more loving place if people actually lived this stuff. I think the world is ready for a big change."

"I'll just stay open to what unfolds in my life, and see what miracles surface," I replied, employing more of Moe's philosophy on life. "It'll all work out the way it's meant to," I added with a knowing smile.

When I landed in New York, Cal's directions led me right to the heart of the financial district and into one of the city's most prestigious office towers. It was an address of distinction, home to international conglomerates and world-class enterprises. I felt a little intimidated as I a boarded an elevator to the 53rd floor, where I was to meet the next guide my father had assigned to me. I'd met Father Mike, a saint of sorts in the way he viewed and conducted his noble life. I'd met Moe Jackson, a cool dude who had taught me about matters of the heart and the importance of staying loose to the moments of my world. Now I had a feeling I'd be learning lessons that would help me raise my career and professional dimension to an entirely new level. My heart began to beat quickly, for I knew that the final phase of my adventure was about to begin.

The elevator door opened, and I stepped into the most stylish suite of offices I'd ever seen. The view from the floor-to-ceiling windows was spectacular, and the furniture was modern chic. It was only 7:45, but handsome men in finely cut suits and lovely women in custom-tailored outfits strode by quickly, exuding enormous confidence and a single-minded purpose.

"Jack, welcome to New York!" a sweet but confident voice called out from the end of a long hallway that was lined with Japanese sculptures and Native American art.

As I turned in the direction of the voice, I saw a stunningly beautiful woman dressed in an expensive black business suit walking directly toward me. Her porcelain skin glowed, her face radiated great warmth, and her eyes sparkled. Her jet black hair was tied into a knot that allowed her face to be the center of attention. And that smile—1,000 watts of pure charisma.

As she grew closer to me, I sensed extraordinary power radiating from her. I couldn't tell you why I experienced this feeling, I just did. It was the same type of sensation I'd had in the past when I'd met a Hollywood star on the street or a sports celebrity in an airport. This woman was the kind of person who stopped a room the moment she entered it—I knew there weren't many like her.

"Jack," she said with polite efficiency as she reached me and shook my hand, "I'm Tess Welch, CEO of this brokerage firm. Your father was a dear friend of mine."

"He was?" I muttered, still captivated by her looks and the dazzling energy she radiated.

"Yes, he was. I miss him very much," she paused. "And I'm so sorry for your loss," she said gently. "Just before he died, he told me that you were coming. He planned all of this for you. My God, he must have loved you. Anyway, how are you doing?"

"Well, it's been a pretty amazing couple of months," I replied. "My time in Rome was unbelievably rewarding—it changed the way I see the world, to be honest. And Hawaii was incredible. The whole thing's been like a dream. My entire life's been turned upside down in so many ways."

"That's not necessarily a bad thing, is it, Jack? From what I heard from Cal, you were due for some wholesale changes," she said in an empathetic way.

"That's true, Ms. Welch," I replied with formality, feeling a little uncomfortable in these sleek surroundings. I wore nothing more than shorts, a T-shirt, and my trusty old sandals, and my backpack was slung over my shoulder.

She smiled. "Please call me Tess. Everyone around here does.

Anyway, I'm delighted that you've made it. I've booked you a room at Morgan's, a really hip hotel that's one of my favorites. Don't worry about a thing. I promised Cal I'd take great care of you, and I'm always true to my word."

"So what will we be focusing on for these next four weeks, Tess?"

"I'll be your career, leadership, and life-legacy coach—I'll teach you all about the third of The Final Questions."

"How to serve greatly?" I recalled.

"Yes. I'll teach you how to live a life that matters; how to shift from simply striving for success to creating lasting *significance*; how to manifest your heart's desires in the physical dimension while building fulfillment in your psychic dimension; and how to realize your potential in your career and grow into greatness. And I'll show you the importance of value creation and why the main aim in business is to selflessly serve."

"This is all exactly what I need to learn at this stage of the game," I replied. "I've learned a lot over the past weeks about inner success—now I feel I'm ready to translate some of those concepts into my career. I think I've made some poor choices along my professional path, and I do feel very unfulfilled in my work."

"Life is all about choices, Jack. As Einstein said: 'How many people are trapped in their everyday habits: part numb, part frightened, part indifferent? To have a better life we must keep choosing how we are living.'"

"What a great quote. I love the lesson that 'we must keep choosing how we are living.' I guess that's what we all need to do as human beings in every moment of our lives—keep choosing our best thinking and our best actions," I stated philosophically, impressing myself with the wisdom that had begun to flow out of me over the past weeks.

"You're quite right. And the choices we make in each one of our moments ultimately add up to the kind of lives we create for ourselves," Tess said as she pointed to an elegantly framed lithograph in the waiting room. "Here's an even better quote by business philosopher Peter Koestenbaum: 'Some people are more talented than others. Some people are more educationally privileged than others. But we all have the capacity to be great. Greatness comes by recognizing that your potential is limited only by how you choose, how you use your freedom, how resolute you are, how persistent you are—in short, by your attitude. And we are all free to choose our attitude.'"

"Neat," I replied, nodding my head and also hoping that she wouldn't notice the particles of sand—happy souvenirs from my month in Hawaii—that my sandals were leaving on the gleaming hardwood floors.

Tess continued our discussion. "We really do need to keep choosing how we live in every moment of our days," she said. "We must keep asking ourselves, 'Is what I'm doing in this instant the best use of my time and talents?' Every moment of our lives is a moment of truth, in a sense. Based on what you choose in each moment, you either grow as a human being or you shrink as one. Who you are right now amounts to nothing more than the sum total of the choices you've made from the day you were born to this day right here. By your choices, you truly will determine your destiny."

"Powerful insight, Tess," I replied.

"The choices that have determined the thoughts that you've habitually thought, the people you've surrounded yourself with, the books you've read, and the actions you've taken have shaped you and defined your life. You've created the life you see before your eyes—no one else has."

"I agree. And I must take complete responsibility for it," I stated confidently, echoing more of Father Mike's wisdom. "Makes me think of what Rudyard Kipling once wrote: 'We have forty million reasons for failure, but not a single excuse.'"

"Brilliant line, Jack. In denying any responsibility for your life by blaming others, you're giving your power away to those people, as I'm sure you know by now. In blaming the things that happened to you in the past or the things that aren't great about your life, you empower those events. Because when you blame the status of your life on other people and things, you're really saying that they've shaped your destiny and are the cause of your current conditions. And that's just not the case."

"*I'm* the cause of everything in my life," I acknowledged. "I've discovered that from all of the reflection I've done over the past eight weeks. I guess the challenge for me is to recognize this, but balance it with the need to be gentle with myself. I really don't want to start beating myself up over all the mistakes I've made along the path of my life."

"Wise point. It *is* a balance."

"But I also need to be real," I added.

"Right. And the realness comes from taking responsibility. Circumstances don't *define* a person, Jack, they *reveal* a person. My point is this: I think that it's time to take back custody of your life. I think you're ready to demand more of yourself, to live by more inspired standards."

"More inspired standards?"

"Yes. It's time for Jack Valentine to start acting like an impeccable human being and *become* one. Here, read this," Tess said as she handed me what appeared to be a business card. "I keep this in my wallet, and I read it every time I open it—this helps me stay centered on what I want my life to stand for. Go ahead, read it aloud."

"'One of the saddest experiences which can come to a

human being is to awaken, grey-haired and wrinkled, near the close of an unproductive career, to the fact that all through the years he has been using only a small part of himself.' — V. W. Burrows." I looked up at Tess with amazement, really feeling the impact of the words I'd read.

"See what I'm saying, Jack? Life is really short. Now is the time to raise your standards about what it means to be a person, to show the world who you really are. And if not now, when?"

That last question really resonated with me. It was as if my head snapped back and the force of the question pinned me against the glass wall of Tess's sophisticated waiting room. I'd always put off doing the things I needed to do to be truly successful in the world until a later date. I'd tell myself that I'd go the extra mile and become a star at work when I had more time. I'd rebuild my relationship once I got promoted. I'd improve my life when I made more money.

But that thinking didn't work for me anymore—it didn't suit my new state of awareness. I really needed to take my life to its highest level. Not next year. Not next month. Not next week. *Now.* My life had already been transformed through my visit with Father Mike and my time with Moe. The way I was thinking, acting, and feeling these days confirmed that I was essentially a new person. But I knew that there was still more of me to discover. Much more. I had to raise my standards and commit to going all the way. I could no longer shrink from my greatness—I owed that to Father Mike and Moe. I thought about what the philosopher Baltasar Gracian once said: "The wise man always does at once what the fool does at finally."

Tess interrupted my thoughts. "You know, Jack, it's so easy to fall into the trap of a mediocre life. If we don't take charge of our lives and act on them, our lives have a way of acting on us. And then the days slip into weeks, the weeks slip into months, and the months slip into years. Before we know it, it's all over! I think it was Nietzsche who challenged us to stop living life as if it were a thoughtless accident. We need to captain *and* pilot our lives in new directions if we desire meaningful success. We need to develop better habits and think bigger thoughts."

"I've been changing a lot of my habits lately."

"That's wonderful! Our habits make us. And the consequences of our bad habits often don't show up until many years later, so we lose sight of how to run our lives. The chickens always come home to roost, and the salmon always return home to spawn."

"Huh?"

"*Actions always have consequences—always.* Do good things for yourself and others in your life, and good things are certain to flow back to you. Treat yourself poorly and fall into the trap of bad habits, and you're bound to pay the price. No matter what you might try to kid yourself into thinking, the chickens always come home to roost."

Tess continued speaking as she paced the grand lobby we were still standing in. "Elite performance in career and in life is all about the promotion of personal accountability. It's about keeping the pledges you've made to yourself. It's essential to honor your self-promises to live an honorable life. Greatness as a person is mostly about saying what we'll do as people, and then doing what we said we would. This is simple stuff, yet most of us have forgotten it in this crazy world we live in."

"After taking full responsibility over my life and honoring my promises, what else should I be thinking about?"

"Be there for the people in your life, Jack, that's most important. Genuinely care about people. Do the unexpected for them, and give them some of yourself. All of us in the corporate world need to stop being so worried about being successful or prosperous or respected—we need to be far more concerned with *being good*. That's the focus that will take us toward our ideal lives. It makes me sad when I see the way so many people in business operate. It's all about 'What's in it for me?' which is a really shortsighted way to conduct a professional life."

"That's precisely how I used to operate at work," I told her. "But no more. That isn't the way I'm going to do things when I get back home. I also want to be more *human* in how I show up as a businessperson."

"Excellent. It's only when you take off that suit of armor that most of us wear all day and show some vulnerability, openness, and caring that your life will move up into the heavens. The best leaders expose their weaknesses—they're real and people love them for it. Being open, decent, and congruent in business is a huge competitive advantage these days. It will really set you apart from the competition and cement the loyalty of your customers."

"It will?"

"Sure—because no one does this anymore!" she said passionately. "Yet all great leaders know this. You'll be so much happier when you learn to authentically be with the people of your life and build extraordinary relationships with them. Release your self-protection and *really* give yourself to others. It will be one of the finest decisions you'll ever make, Jack."

"I haven't really been there for the people in my life, Tess. It makes me feel bad to think about the way I've treated others."

"If you show them that you value them, they'll come to value you. Shower them with love and concern, and they'll shower *you* with love and concern. Ask about their hopes, dreams, and desires, and they'll do the same for you. Great lives—both at work and at home—are built upon great relationships, you know."

"That makes perfect sense."

"Did you know that recent scientific evidence has shown that the electromagnetic field created by the human heart is actually 5,000 times more powerful than the one created by the human mind?"

"I had no idea," I replied, surprised at the breadth of this remarkable woman's knowledge.

"What this translates into, according to the scientific evidence, is this: People can actually *feel* that field five to ten feet away from you. Can you see how important this finding is?"

"Other people can feel if you care about them, so they can truly know whether or not you have their best interests at heart. Extraordinary."

"Exactly. It means that no matter how smart you think you are, you can't fake caring. You can talk the talk all you want, but unless you're genuinely devoted to helping your clients and making their lives better, they won't do business with you—they'll sense that you're not genuine. Success in business comes down to trust, Jack. People need to trust that you want to help them. If the trust is there, your services will sell themselves."

"Is trust really that important?" I asked. "I mean, I've heard that things such as quality of goods, service levels, and innovation are what really makes for success in business."

"Trust is where it all begins. People do business with people they trust. Let's say you had a heart attack, God forbid. Would you rather go to a surgeon that you trust completely or one that had a great reputation but was untrustworthy?"

"I'd go to the one I trusted, as long as I felt he could do a great job."

"Of course you would," Tess said. "Trust is the defining advantage that the surgeon has, and it's the cornerstone of every strong businesses relationship. Without trust, your prospects won't buy from you, your teammates won't listen to you, and your family and friends will run away from you."

"Trust is key," I confirmed.

"It truly is, Jack. Without it, your relationships are nothing more than shells of what they could be. And you maintain a trust account with every person in your life. Whenever you interact with someone, you're either making deposits into that account or withdrawing from it. Every time you follow through on a commitment you've made, every time you take a moment to say 'thank you,' every time you show real interest in someone, and every time you authentically help another is a deposit."

"And every time I put myself first is a withdrawal."

"Yes. Each time you fail to do what you said you'd do, neglect to return a phone call, speak poorly about someone behind their back, or fail to deliver a high-quality product, you're making withdrawals. Daily deposits deepen the relationship, while daily withdrawals diminish it. And the interesting thing is that when you have a lot invested in that trust account, you can make a few withdrawals without too much of a problem."

"It's almost like I have credit."

"Or overdraft protection," Tess said with a gentle smile. "And it works like this in your personal life as well. Let's say, for example, that there's a special woman you've been dating. You've always picked her up for your dates on time, you've always called her when you said you would, you've shown her great care and attention, and you've helped her when she's asked for your help. In other words, you have good credit in that trust account. So if you have to cancel a date or two because there's an urgent matter that's come up at work, what do you think her response would be?"

"She'd be fine with it. I'd think she'd support me if an emergency came up."

"Right, because of all of those deposits you've made. Now

let's alter the scenario: Say that you've established a pattern of missing dates, you haven't called her when you promised you would, and you've forgotten a few important occasions."

"I'm getting the picture—I've made far too many withdrawals."

"Yes. Now, one day you call her up and tell her you need to cancel the next few dates you've set up because of some crisis at work. What do you guess her response would be?"

"She probably wouldn't be impressed. In fact, if she took it badly, it might even be enough for her to throw in the towel and leave the relationship."

"You got it. So do you see how we all need to make frequent deposits in the trust accounts of everyone we're in relationship with—not just in our business lives but within our personal lives, too?"

"Yes, I do. And a great way to do that is to be caring and kind, right?"

"That's it, Jack. Consistent caring and true kindness is so very powerful—especially in a business context, where people are so busy that they've forgotten how to treat people. I look for every opportunity to show and tell my team that I love them."

"You tell your team you love them?"

"Yes. And I really do. I think about them all the time. These people have given some of the best years of their lives to help me grow this enterprise. I honor them for that. Their successes are my successes, and their setbacks are my setbacks."

Tess then folded her hands together in the traditional greeting of people from India as she stood in the center of the waiting area. Smart-looking executives continued to stride by, and I could see the skyline of New York through the massive windows. Tess's pose didn't seem to match her surroundings, so I asked her what she was doing.

175

"I learned this when I was on a trip to Southeast Asia a few years ago. This is how the citizens of India greet each other," she said, clasping her hands together. "Namaste."

"What does that mean?"

"It means, 'I honor the best and highest within you.' Isn't that a wonderful way to greet someone, Jack? Could you imagine how you'd feel about your life and how others would feel about you if every time you met someone you honored the best and the highest within them? Now I'm not saying that you need to perform this ritual outwardly—but you could easily express the sentiment silently every time someone crossed your path. As science confirms, at a deep, invisible level, they'd feel the goodwill that you have for them. And this would cause them to treat you in ways that reflect the best within themselves."

"The way this works is fascinating," I replied, absorbed with what this business superstar was telling me about the conduct of an extraordinary professional life.

"So when you meet someone, just take a second and remind yourself to honor the goodness within them. Lock in an appreciation for them as the magnificent human creatures that they are. It will make a profound difference in the way they respond to you. And you'll feel more fulfilled in your work and in your life as a whole. You know, when I walk past my teammates here, I always silently appreciate the wonders they are. And that has made a world of difference in terms of our connection."

A trendy young receptionist broke in. "Tess, there's an extremely important call for you from Geneva on line one. I know you asked not to be disturbed while you met with Mr. Valentine, but this seems to be something of an emergency."

"No problem, Summer—I'll take the call in my office," replied Tess warmly. "Jack, we're working on a massive deal, and things have gotten a little off track. Just give me 15 minutes or so, and I'll be right back. In the meantime, relax and make yourself comfortable. Summer here will get you a nice glass of fresh orange juice if you like. Sorry about this."

As Tess strode down the hallway, I sat down to collect my thoughts. My eyes happened upon a book, titled *A Calendar of Wisdom*. It was a treasury of sacred quotes compiled by the great Russian novelist Leo Tolstoy. I opened the book and read the first quote that caught my eye. Although it was a simple statement, it spoke deeply to me:

"Life is short. Do not forget about the most important things in life, living for other people and doing good for them."

12 LOVE AS A BUSINESS TOOL

"Keep the gold and keep the silver, but give us wisdom."

— Arabian proverb

———— ✦ ————

"Jack, there are only two states a human being can be in at any given moment: fear or love," Tess told me when she returned from her conference call.

"Moe taught me that in Hawaii," I replied.

"I figured he would. Moe's an extremely wise man. Trust what he taught you."

I was surprised. "You know Moe?"

She nodded. "He's a great friend of mine. Anyway, it's true that, in any given moment, you're either living in fear or you're living in love. And I choose not to live my life in fear because it limits me and the life I'm dedicated to creating. Every moment of every day, my conscious choice is that of love. And that's one of the deepest secrets of my success."

"Love as a business strategy. Pretty cool, Tess, pretty cool."

"You know, Jack, you can get everything you want out of life when you focus on helping those around you get everything *they* want out of life."

"I like that one."

"My life changed when I made a simple decision and set a new standard for myself: *to become the most caring person I knew.* Try setting that inspired standard for yourself and see what happens. It's the one thing in my life that I've attached a 'no exceptions policy' to. It doesn't matter what intervenes, I'll always put that value above all else. I'm deeply dedicated to being the most caring person I know—it's almost as if I've written that onto my heart."

Tess took a deep breath and went on. "This company generated over a billion dollars in revenue last year. But what made me even happier was seeing the successes of the men and woman that are this company. When they grow as human beings through the work they do, I grow as a person. What really fills me up, more than almost anything else, is seeing my employees turn into leaders and happy people who feel that they're contributing and doing their part to make the world a better place. What really inspires me is watching how our company's culture has developed into one where people truly are number one, and creating a workplace where it's safe to be human again. I'm far more fulfilled by the quality of my relationships with my employees, clients, and suppliers than by the amount of cash in my bank account."

"Wow! You definitely operate under a very different set of business standards," I remarked with genuine respect.

"I know," Tess replied.

She then took out a gold case from the pocket of her suit jacket and opened it.

"Here," she said as she handed me a card, "read this. My title shows people what I stand for."

Tess's business card had silver embossed lettering on it,

which I could tell was very expensive. Her name appeared at the top, and underneath it was her title. It said: "C.L.O."

"What does C.L.O. mean, Tess? I would have expected C.E.O.," I noted.

"C.L.O. is short for 'Chief Love Officer,'" she said with a laugh. "Of course I only use these cards in special situations—I have more conventional business cards in my office. But the fact is, here at this firm, I see my role as Chief Love Officer. I'm here to show my team I care about them and that I love them.'

"Very unique," was all I could say.

"I know it is—that's probably why I'm the happiest person I know in a market that sees most top executives unhappy, unfulfilled, and empty. Did you know that one of the most powerful cures that psychiatrists prescribe for business executives who come to them suffering from depression is a daily dose of friendship?"

"Seriously?"

"Yes. You see, Jack, most of these executives live their lives in ivory towers—they spend their days in isolation. And as a consequence, the human need that we all have for a bond with a community isn't satisfied."

"So the psychiatrists tell them to go out and make friends?"

"That's almost exactly it. They tell the executives to go out and befriend other people, to be concerned over the welfare of others, to laugh and share stories with those they work and live with, and to open their hearts to others. And it works. It was all written up in a great article entitled "The Human Moment at Work," which appeared in the *Harvard Business Review*."

"Remarkable, Tess. And the idea is so simple."

"Yes, it is. So, in terms of your own career, what I'm suggesting is that you truly *be* for people. Be far more concerned about deepening your relationships than making the sale . . . and the sales will automatically make themselves. Massive success in business really is all about human connections."

"What exactly are human connections?"

"They're the bonds that link us, person to person. Human connections occur when we genuinely try to serve other people and make a difference in their lives—when we learn how to communicate from the heart, speak our truth, and sincerely become empathetic listeners, getting behind the eyeballs of those we're listening to in an effort to understand them. Communication is so essential to showing leadership in your career."

"That's interesting, Tess. One of the new goals I've set for myself is to be an excellent communicator. I really want to make a special effort to show people that I cherish and understand them. I know it will help me in my career."

"Yes. And it's just the *right* thing to do. As you know, we're not on the planet all that long. Why not make our time here enjoyable by enjoying the people around us? Get good at conversations."

"What do you mean by that?"

"One of the most essential lessons I've learned along my path is that a great life is nothing more than a series of great conversations. Business success comes from having thoughtful conversations with our teammates, customers, and prospects. If we stop engaging in these conversations, we lose the business. Family success comes from having meaningful conversations with our mates and among our children. Lose these conversations, and we lose the family. And inner success—success as a human being—involves, in many ways, nothing more than a continual conversation and connection with your highest self. Lose that conversation, and you lose yourself."

"That's a brilliant insight."

"Thank you, Jack. So many people in our world today are divorced from themselves. They've become so busy chasing fame and acclaim that they've stopped conversing with themselves at a deep inner level. You know, one of the most important things that any leader can do is to deepen themselves. The deeper you get, the more you'll wake up to what the voyage of life is all about. And the more you awaken, the more you'll realize that success is all about making a difference in the world. Oh, that brings up another important point," Tess added. "If you hope to manifest abundance in your life and succeed in your career, it's essential to become a value builder."

"What's that?"

"The elite performers in life spend their time centered on creating and building value rather than on making money. They seek out ways to enrich others, and they live to improve the lot of those who have the privilege of doing business with them. They take themselves out of the equation and exist, in many ways, for others. The irony is that they're the ones who become the most successful and wealthy."

"Really?" I asked.

"Yes, really. To have more in the world, you must give more to others. It's just one of those timeless laws of life."

"I've been hearing a lot about those lately."

"Well, that's good." Tess smiled. "Always be asking yourself the questions: 'How can I add value to this person?' and 'How can I serve the world today?' You'll be rewarded with extraordinary abundance. Martin Luther King, Jr., said it so well when he stated: 'Life's most persistent and urgent question is what are you doing for others?'"

"Powerful words," I noted.

Tess began to walk down the long corridor. "Jack," she said, "please follow me."

She led me into a large room with gleaming hardwood floors and a series of rich leather chairs with glass tables beside them. On the walls were shelves full of books. I studied the titles: *The Art of Living,* by Epictetus; *The Meditations of Marcus Aurelius; Think and Grow Rich,* by Napoleon Hill; There was even an oddly titled little book called *The Monk Who Sold His Ferrari,* which brought a smile to my face.

"This is our firm's learning lounge," Tess said as she poured herself a cup of herbal tea. "Want some? It tastes great with honey."

"Sure," I replied.

"Anyway, this room is where we all come to think. Elite performers in business make a lot of time to reflect. And one of the things they think about the most is how they can add more value to the people they serve. You know, most people have it all wrong," Tess observed.

"They do?" I asked.

"Yes. The purpose of life isn't to be happy. That's one of the most self-centered ways of living that one could imagine, and it's the source of so many problems in the world today. This global community would change if we'd stop thinking about our individual happiness and start to think about our collective service. In other words, the word would change if we began to become consumed, not with being happier, but with being more valuable. To get to the next level of our lives, Jack, the question isn't, 'How can I have more?' The question really is, 'How can I *be* more?' Stop wishing that life were easier and wish that *you* were better, more caring, and more kind. Stop wishing for fewer problems and wish for greater wisdom. You see, happiness is a by-product, and it comes to those who don't seek it."

"It's a paradox, isn't it?" I observed.

"Yes, in many ways, it is. I really think that the more you

seek happiness and success, the more it will run away from you. Happiness and success are the unintended yet inevitable by-products of a life spent creating value for other human beings. Do that, and everything else will fall into place exactly as it should."

"So most businesses today have it wrong. The goal isn't to make money—"

"It's to make meaning," Tess interjected. "The primary objective of business is to help those you serve find greater meaning, joy, and success in their lives through the products and services that you offer to them. Of course, making money is very important, but it shouldn't be the primary driver if you're looking for true success. Good companies focus purely on profit; *great* companies focus on their higher purpose—to create great results for their customers and make a difference in their lives."

"That's the first time I've ever heard anything like this."

"Look, I'm in business to make money—please don't get me wrong. I'm not some idealist with no sense of the way the real world operates. I have an MBA from Harvard Business School and a Ph.D. from Stanford. I've spent most of my adult life here on Wall Street, and I play the game of business at the highest of levels. Money buys freedom to some degree, I know that. The best thing you can do to help the poor of this world is to ensure that you're not one of them. And to be honest, Jack, I've personally made a ton of money—millions and millions for sure. You get to a point where you really don't know how much money you have; it's just not an issue anymore. I can have whatever I want whenever I want it. But from an early point, all money was for me was a means of keeping track, a scorecard of sorts."

"For keeping track of what?"

"Of the amount of value I create. I've found that the more

value I create in the world, the more the money seems to roll into my life. Money has no value per se, does it?"

"I guess you're right. It's just paper."

"Yes. All money is is a symbol of a value exchange. To me, it only gets its value when I *deliver* my value. It's only a yardstick to me, nothing more, nothing less. So my point is this: Money's important, but it's definitely not my central motivator. Money isn't what gets me out of bed at five in the morning, and it isn't what pushes me to innovate and be the best in the world at everything I do. I'd rather be paid in psychic rewards instead of monetary rewards, for they make me feel good about myself as a human being. I get my meaning not from money but from service. I live to help others. That's what really motivates me—a sense of mission and meaning, not money and material rewards. And that's where so many other companies go wrong—they focus more on amassing wealth than on helping other people fulfill their dreams."

Tess then walked me to her office. It was impeccably elegant, furnished in a modern minimalist style. Her splendid view looked out over the entire city. Pictures of her husband and three children were everywhere.

"Jack, try to live by the words of Woodrow Wilson: 'You are not here to make a living. You are here in order to enable the world to live more amply, with greater vision, with a finer spirit of hope and achievement. You are here to enrich the world and you impoverish yourself if you forget that errand.'"

"Profound lines."

"And when you serve, do it without any expectation of reward. If you help another person at work, whether it's coming to the aid of a colleague trying to learn a new computer process or serving a customer by dazzling her with your willingness to ensure your product is exactly what she needs, do it for the pure joy of giving. Giving with the intention of receiving really isn't giving, it's trading—and people can sense that. Give to genuinely help, and act like a servant leader. That's how you'll grow to greatness."

"What's a servant leader?"

"The best leaders are servant leaders. All they care about is serving their constituents. Their lives reflect a sense of mission— it's what drives them and fuels their days."

"That's a fantastic way to live!" I said excitedly. "Finding a mission that you can give yourself over to, and then pending your days moving that mission forward."

"Precisely," Tess replied. "Think of Mahatma Gandhi, Nelson Mandela, and Mother Teresa, as well as the greatest religious leaders of history. All were servant leaders, and all had a dedication to a cause greater than themselves—a mission."

"And this mission needs to be about serving others, right?"

"It must. But you don't have to set your sights on transforming the world to live with a sense of mission. Your call might be to serve your customers at work with love, decency, and a great commitment to creating value in their businesses. That aim is no less noble than changing the world. Even if your job was to sweep streets or pick up garbage, you have the choice to work with a sense of mission and an ethic of service, seeing it as an opportunity to make the community a better place. There are no small jobs, Jack. Mahatma Gandhi said it so well when he observed: 'No matter how insignificant the thing you have to do, do it as well as you can, give it as much of your care and attention as you would give to the thing you regard as most important. For it will be by those small things that you shall be judged.'"

"Beautiful point, Tess."

"And it was Mother Teresa who said: 'Let no one ever come

to you without leaving better and happier.'"

"Great words."

"I also love the words of William Penn, who said: 'I expect to pass through life but once. If, therefore, there be any kindness I can show, or any good thing I can do to any fellow being, let me do it now, and not defer or neglect it, as I shall not pass this way again.' Once you live by this philosophy, it will change radically for the better—this I promise you," Tess said intensely.

"See, that's one of the reasons I love work," she continued. "I can fulfill one of the deepest needs of every human being through the way I work."

"Which is?"

"The need for self-transcendence. We all have an enormous longing within us, at a primary level, to make a difference in the world. I believe we've all been programmed to contribute to the world in our own special way—it's in our genetic makeup. For some, it will be leading countries to freedom and touching the lives of millions; for others, it will be sweeping streets or working at the checkout stand of a local convenience store. As I'm saying, no pursuit is no better or more worthy of our respect than another if it's performed with our whole hearts and with a sense of duty. As the thinker John Ruskin put it: 'The weakest among us has a gift, however seemingly trivial, which is peculiar to him and which worthily used will be a gift also to his race.'"

"I feel those words in my heart," I said sincerely.

"That's because they speak to the best within you, Jack. The truth of these words resonates with the place of *knowing* within you. The deepest need of the human heart, when you get right down to it, is the need to live for something more important than ourselves. You might not realize that now. You might feel uneasy hearing that because your dream is to make a ton of cash and buy a home in the Caymans. Or you might dismiss this point in a world centered on 'looking out for Number One.' But Jack, I have to tell you that the more you get to the truth of what life is all about, and the deeper you go into your natural wisdom, the more one truth will be inescapable: *An impeccable life is created when you serve impeccably.* The more inner work you do on yourself as a human being, the more you'll come to see the world in a very different way. You won't be so plugged in to needing to make a lot of money so that other people will respect you. You'll be so focused on your higher mission that your self-respect will carry the day. We're all meant to be leaders on the planet—it's our birthright."

Tess then pointed to a quote that had literally been carved by a skilled craftsperson directly onto the top of her desk.

"Read this," she said. "It keeps me focused each morning. Sometimes I read these words, and then I close my eyes and feel them being drawn into my heart. It's a cool meditation I do, and it makes a wonderful impact on the way I live out my day."

The words were as follows:

"You will be happy in your life in direct proportion to the degree to which you will be helpful to the world."

13 THE REAL WAY TO SUCCEED

"Death is not the greatest loss in life. The greatest loss is what dies inside us while we live."

— Norman Cousins

——— ✦ ———

As we sat down on a leather sofa stationed in her office, Tess said, "It's not where you end up in your career that's important—it's what the journey you've taken to get to that place makes of you as a human being. The true reward of a well-lived life doesn't lie in what you get at the end of your path, but what you become once you get there."

"Amazing insight," I remarked.

"It's the *process* of your life that's the key to your life, not where you finally rest at the end of the day. Success really doesn't lie in reaching your goals—it lies in the personal transformations and inner shifts in consciousness that take place as necessary consequences of advancing toward your goals. It's not making the goal happen that's the gift, but what getting to that particular goal makes of you as a person. And frankly, I believe that there are only two reasons to be in business."

I waited for her to continue.

"First, as I've mentioned, to create value for others and for the benefit of the greater good; and second, to grow as a person. To actualize who we really are and, in doing so, make peace with ourselves," she said.

"When we finally discover who we truly are, we make peace with ourselves?"

"Yes. This is the best way to live a rich and peaceful life."

"That makes so much sense, Tess. Maybe many of our struggles as human beings happen because the deepest part of us knows that we're betraying ourselves by not living our lives to their highest potential."

"That's it exactly. We lose an enormous amount of respect for ourselves when we fail to actualize our highest human potential. We think it takes a lot of energy to do the inner work required to live our best lives, both at work and at home—the reality is that it takes far more energy to stay mediocre."

"I'd agree with that."

"There's no question that it's extremely draining to deny your dreams and neglect the path of your best life. It takes a lot of energy to not be true to yourself."

"Okay, I hear where you're coming from. I'm feeling very inspired by this conversation, Tess. I really see the importance of loving others and making human connections. I'll commit, right here and right now to becoming a man who lives far more for others. And I also promise you that I'll begin to view myself as a value builder. I'm going to build my career based not on what I can get from others but what I can be for others." I smiled. "I should tell you that just saying that makes me feel much better about my career. I'll also begin to live at a much higher level."

"That's wonderful," she replied, clearly pleased by my comments.

"But let me play devil's advocate on the issue of giving yourself to others for a moment. I'm sure you'll agree that there are some truly ruthless and mean people out there."

"I'll agree that there are some people out there whose *behavior* is ruthless and mean."

"Okay, I see the distinction. But when you're dealing with such people, surely you can't always be loving."

"I *always* choose to be loving, Jack. That's the standard I live my life by, and it works for me. But—and this is a very important point—being loving doesn't mean being weak. A wise human being blends compassion with courage."

"Oh?"

"Yes. That's the principle I live under. Sometimes circumstances dictate that I express my love via compassion, and at other times they call for me to be courageous. People make the mistake of believing that to be loving means you have to give in to people and let them walk all over you. That's just not the case. I love myself too much to ever let that happen. If someone crosses the boundary with me, I let them know it in a compassionate yet powerful way. I speak in a way that doesn't sting them but lets them know that I won't be mistreated. And so, I blend compassion with courage. You know, Jack, we teach people how to treat us."

"We do?"

"Absolutely. If someone in your life is treating you harshly, without the respect that you deserve, then in some way I can assure you that you've permitted that to happen. Perhaps when they were first rude to you, you failed to set a boundary and didn't tell them that this was unacceptable. And this failure taught them that they could get away with their less-than-respectful behavior."

"So every single person in my life has been taught how to

treat me by the way I let them treat me?"

"That's it. Expect and ensure that you're treated with courtesy, care, and love, and that's what you'll get. Allow people to walk all over you, and you'll be educating them in that technique and holding them to this lower standard."

"I understand." I thought for a moment. "And what are your thoughts about competition? You're in one of the most competitive industries in the world—financial services—and you're clearly a huge success. How can a person who's highly loving thrive in our world? Can I really be successful if I don't try to win?"

"Actually, if you only try to win, I can guarantee you that you won't be successful at all," Tess said with a laugh. "As CEO of this organization, I have to think about market share and keep one eye on the competition at all times. That's a given in this economy we operate in. But many years ago, after a year-long sabbatical where I sailed around the world with my family, I began to open the aperture through which I see the world. My worldview changed dramatically in my self-imposed exile of sorts." She smiled.

"Jack, you've heard some of the organizing principles I've built my new life on. I'll share another one as it relates to your question about competition: *For you to win, no one needs to lose.* Now that's a hard one for many of us in the business world to swallow. After all, even as kids we're conditioned to compete for scarce resources. We're told to be best in our classes at school and encouraged to be first in the sports we perform. We're constantly compared to others who we're told are better, smarter, and faster. What this does is create a scarcity mind-set, and we begin to believe that the world really is a place with limited resources. If we don't graduate at the top of our class, we won't succeed in our careers. If we don't win in sports, we'll never taste victory.

Now this is all false thinking—nothing could be further from the truth. The philosopher Rumi made the point well when he observed: 'Give up the drop. Become the ocean.'"

"That one just sent a shiver down my back, Tess."

She continued. "And this false thinking originates fear—fear that there's not enough in the world for every one of us to succeed beyond our wildest expectations; fear that we'll lose what we've struggled so hard to accumulate; fear that we don't deserve to keep what we have. And this fear sets up an interesting situation: The more we fear that we'll lose if we help others win, the less we end up having. The more we try to hoard, the more we push away the abundance that's due to us."

"How could that be?"

"Because our thinking defines our reality—our perception determines our experience. If all you think about is having everything for yourself and not helping others get to their dreams, then you're projecting your fears out into the world. And those fear-filled thoughts will create your reality, so you'll live a life of lack."

"Do you mean to say that by thinking only about ourselves and trying to own everything, we actually lose?"

"Yes. It's hard to believe, isn't it? Here's the key—every single person on the planet is connected. We're all cut from the same cloth. All competition does is fuel the illusion that we're all separate, which keeps one of us small. When we operate at a higher level and begin to see the interconnectedness of everything, we all win. The world wins. When your main aim is to enrich others and support them as they grow into who they're destined to be, you send abundant thoughts out into the world rather than projecting fear."

"And so the world floods our lives with abundance," I mused.

"Exactly. The fact of the matter is that our world has never had so many opportunities available to those who seek them out. We all can win here. And if we all work together, in a state of cooperation and harmony, then the entire world will become a better place to be. But constantly striving to beat the competition breeds tremendous stress—you fall into the performance trap and begin thinking that you'll only be admired if you win. That sets up an interesting pattern of action in our lives."

"Which is?"

"We become obsessed with outperforming others. We become like circus animals, performing in the hope of receiving acclaim from others. We base our self-worth on receiving praise from those we care about and, therefore, we keep pushing ourselves relentlessly. But *nothing* can ever be enough when we live like this. We meet one big goal but are so busy climbing the imaginary ladder of success that we can't enjoy the accomplishment. Nothing is ever enough for us when we have this kind of a belief setup. Nothing is ever good enough because we must be number one."

"It almost sounds like perfectionism."

"That's exactly what it is. We're trying to be perfect. And we destroy our souls in the process."

"Okay. So what's the solution?"

"Trust and relax more."

Father Mike told me to trust more—and so did Moe. They both believed that the universe is a friendly place, and no matter what happens to us as we journey through our lives, it will all work out in a beautiful way. As a matter of fact, it seemed that the more I stopped my frenzied struggling and trusted that the world worked in a way that wanted me to succeed, the more the world would deliver its rewards to me. Interesting . . . the less I pushed, the more I'd get. In many ways, I wanted the laws of the world that Father Mike and Moe had taught me to prove themselves before I embraced them—I didn't realize that I had to first embrace them before they'd prove themselves to me.

It was all about trust. Trusting in the exquisite design of the world and in this highly intelligent plan for our lives. Our lives, I was learning, have been designed to work. We just need to get out of our own way. The more I thought about it, the more I realized that this was amazing stuff.

"Fearing competition makes us wary of others, Jack. That's no way to work or live. Being afraid of losing shuts down our creativity, limits the possibilities of our lives, creates enormous amounts of pressure, and induces tension in our bodies. So ironically, fighting the competition actually diminishes the levels at which we perform, rather than elevating them. The solution is simple: Focus only on being the best *you* can be. Then the only thing you'll have to compare yourself to is the person that you used to be, your former self. Keep examining who you were and where you want to be. Keep moving ahead on the personal odyssey that is a life."

"Tess, I need to be honest with you. I'm afraid that if I don't compete and seize every opportunity in business to win, I'll end up as the big loser. The philosophy you're sharing sounds great but, to be really candid with you, it seems fairly idealistic."

"Thanks for being so honest, Jack. I built this entire business from scratch on this win-win philosophy—and the company's worth millions today. You've really got to trust me that it'll work. Also keep in mind that for hundreds if not thousands of years, people in business have operated from this fear-based, competitive mind-set. And look where it's gotten us as a global community—look at what the work looks like, and the lack of caring and love there is. You know that if we keep doing things the same way, we're only going to see the same results."

"True."

"So to change the world, each one of us must exercise a higher form of leadership and do things in a different way. This is a *huge* opportunity for you, Jack—you can be a leader in the world, in your own special way, by refusing to follow the crowd and acting from a position of love versus one of fear. If you go out into your marketplace and dedicate yourself to genuine service, value creation, relationship building, and win-win outcomes in all cases, your life cannot help but change. The laws of nature have always governed the way life works—watch nature and you'll see a great confirmation of what I'm talking about. *When we work in harmony, there's more for everyone.* That's the biggest lesson for people in business today. And if we fail to get it, the world will become an even messier place."

Tess took a slice of lemon from a plate in silver tray that rested on her credenza and placed it in a glass of water.

"Here, this is for you. Water is good for the brain."

"It is?"

"Of course. It actually helps you think more clearly, especially in times of stress. It's also one of the most effective ways I know of to keep energy levels high." She took a sip from her glass. "Anyway, I want to cover a few quick points before I have to leave you for a meeting."

"I'm really getting a lot from this morning. I'm very grateful for your time, Tess."

"I'm happy to help," she replied. "Just be sure to share what I'm teaching you with others. Our world needs to change, and you can be a powerful catalyst for the transformation of others."

"Okay."

"My most prized asset isn't a material one, you know," Tess added.

"I'm not surprised."

"What's of greatest value to me is my reputation. It never ceases to amaze me how people will work for decades to build a good name, then do something silly, and in a matter of moments, lose their reputation. In doing so, they lose their ability to conduct business in so many ways. You see, Jack, you can't put a price tag on getting your phone calls returned. Cherish your good name. Never do anything that would put a stain on your reputation. Live and work with a great deal of integrity. "

One of the phone lines on Tess's neatly organized desk lit up.

"Oh, that must be about my meeting. Sorry about this, Jack—it's been scheduled for over a month, and I just couldn't cancel it. Here, take this business card," she said quickly. "It's for the hotel you'll be staying in. My driver will take you there, and you can get settled in. I know you must be a little tired from your journey. We've covered a lot in a short time, so the next few days are all about fun for you. I've arranged for one of the best guides in the city to show you around. I'll be in touch in a few days. My home number is on the back of the card—call me if you need anything."

Tess then reached over and gave me a quick hug.

"You're doing great, Jack. I know this is a time of change for you, but don't worry about a thing. My intuition tells me that you're exactly where you need to be on the path of your life. Stay the course and you'll be fine."

With that, Tess Welsh, the superstar CEO, strode out of the room and down the hallway.

—— ✦ ——

14

"The most pathetic person in the world is someone who has sight, but has no vision."

— Helen Keller

———— ✦ ————

The next few days were beautiful—and a celebration of sorts. I'd learned so much in the past weeks that I knew it was important to honor myself for all my growth. I visited art galleries and museums, dined at world-class restaurants, and saw two Broadway plays from the best seats in the house. Tess Welch took care of everything, and arranged for me to be treated like a prince. She was a very kind woman.

Four days after our first meeting, she called me. "Hi, Jack," she said. "I'll meet you in Central Park today so we can walk together for a few hours. There are some lessons I want to share with you that will be very helpful."

An hour later, we were walking through the park, which was filled with New Yorkers taking in the joys of this special place. The brilliant sun shone upon our faces as Tess picked up where she had left off a few days before.

"Jack, if you're really serious about manifesting your heart's desires, there are five simple steps that will make them all happen for you. Trust me on this—these steps work like magic," she assured me.

"I'd love to hear them," I said eagerly.

"The first step is to articulate a vision. Before you can claim what you desire in life, you must *name* what you desire in your life."

"Nice way of putting it."

"The more clarity, color, emotion, and definition you can bring to the goal you've pictured in your imagination, the greater the probability that it will occur in your outer world. You must define your goals—they're nothing more than intentions, and your intentions determine the reality that you create. I've found it extremely helpful to articulate the vision on paper, by the way. Attaching visual words to your desire breathes a life force into it."

"It does?"

"Definitely," came the confident reply.

"Okay, that's easy to do. What's next?"

"Step two is to develop your strategy," Tess informed me. "World-class companies are those who have masterful strategies. You must learn to become very strategic in your life. Always be thinking about what your best life looks like and what you want in your ideal future. Then break that vision down into a strategy to execute it under."

"I'd love to have an ideal future."

"You will, Jack. Your strategy is really your action plan for closing the gap between vision and results. It's your winning formula for bridging your dreams and your actions. The desire you want to manifest in your life begins as nothing more than a vision that appears in your imagination. While that's a beautiful thing, the objective is to translate it into a tangible result—otherwise, what's the point?"

"I agree. Wishful thinking never gets us anywhere."

"Right. Being a leader in your career is all about being proactive. So it's vital that you develop a week-to-week strategy of what you'll do to bridge the gap between the vision and the end result you aspire to. A big dream broken down into manageable segments is far easier to realize."

"It's also less intimidating," I said. "I've found that when a goal is too big, it's often so scary to me that I don't take the first step."

Tess nodded. "I've experienced the same thing in my life. So break down the macro intention down into micro portions. In doing this, your progress will be more graceful, and you'll experience less struggle."

"Got it. What's step three?"

"Set up a self-contract. Make an agreement with yourself stating what you plan to do and when you plan to do it. Print it out from your computer and put a seal on it so it looks official. I even sign mine so it becomes binding, just as if it were a big business deal."

"Is there really value in setting up a self-contract?"

"No question. It puts in place an all-important accountability structure. You see, Jack, without personal accountability, it's easy to escape from your commitment to making the dream happen. Without a structure to ensure that you remain accountable to keeping the promises you've made around manifesting the desire, it's easy to let things slip. Far too many dreams die on the drawing board because of The Law of Diminishing Intent."

"What's that?"

"The Law of Diminishing Intent holds that the more time that passes after you've set a goal, the less likely you are to breathe life into it and make it happen. When we initially set a goal, we tend to be full of excitement and hope about the future possibilities. But as the days pass, life gets in the way, as do our limiting beliefs. Our inner critic begins its work and offers up an array of excuses as to why this goal will never come to fruition. The more time passes, the more we get distracted by the urgent issues we have to deal with—soon the dream dies a quick death. Just imagine if you acted on even 5 percent of the brilliant ideas you've had over the course of your life, not only for success in your career but for success in your life."

"I'd be living at a whole new level," I realized, somewhat sheepishly.

"My point exactly. I've always believed that elite performers never leave the site of a new idea without taking some action to advance it. So to prevent The Law of Diminishing Intent from strangling the desires of your heart, you must build an accountability structure into the process I'm sharing with you. You must have in place some means by which you're held personally accountable to keep following through on the plans you've set. The best way I know of is to engage the services of a coach."

"I've been hearing a lot about coaches these days."

"I'm sure you have," Tess replied. "I've worked with a professional coach every week for the past two years, and she's helped me make profound changes in my life. Not only is she my enthusiastic cheerleader who celebrates my successes, she's also a strict taskmaster of sorts, holding me true to my word and making certain that I do what I say I'll do, when I said I'll do it. The results I've seen in my life have paid for the investment I've made in her services many, many times over."

"What if I can't afford a coach?"

"Well, then the next best thing is to forge a mastermind alliance."

"I'm not familiar with that term," I admitted.

"A mastermind alliance is nothing more than a win-win partnership that you strike with one or more like-minded people to help dreams come true."

"I love the sound of that."

"Here's how I recommend you put this idea into play. Set a time to meet every week, and get together with the members of your alliance as early as possible—meeting early in the morning is important, as it shows commitment. Start the meeting off by revisiting the desires and goals each of you has set for yourselves. Then discuss what's working and what's not. Most important, look at your self-contracts and hold each other accountable for the advancements you each promised you'd make. For this to work, it's important that every member of the group know it's safe to speak their truth and be deeply honest. If you said you'd do something during the preceding week and you've failed to do so, the members of the alliance should be obliged to call you on this. It can be done in a way that's both courageous yet compassionate."

"This is a great idea—it's so simple, yet so powerful."

"To me, manifesting my heart's desires is serious stuff. I don't play games when it comes to creating extraordinary results in my life. I want to live my best life, so I play to win. This five-step process I'm sharing works."

"Okay, so step one is to define my vision; step two involves creating a strategy; step three requires that I set up a self-contract and put in place an accountability structure to ensure that I do what I say I'm going to do. What's next?"

"Step four speaks to measurement. I've always believed that, in business as well as in life, what's not measured will never be mastered. Our business has an incredible array of metrics in place to constantly monitor and measure our progress. When I started this company, I had a simple philosophy. I benchmarked the best companies on the planet and got a very clear picture of the way they operated. And then, even though we started out very small, we dedicated ourselves to operating just like one of those world-class companies each and every day. In the mornings, we'd have a quick huddle and a conversation reminding us what the company we wanted to build would look like. And at the end of the day, we measured what we'd done, in terms of our results, against that idea. Now could you imagine what would happen if you brought this operating strategy into your *life?* What if at the end of every day, you set aside 10 or 15 minutes to measure how you lived out your day against the vision you've set for yourself? Ben Franklin writes about employing this very practice every night in his wonderful autobiography, which you simply must read, by the way. Franklin promised himself that he'd conduct his life under 13 virtues—13 life laws, if you will. Then every night, he would retire to a quiet place and do some deep reflection around how he acted as compared to these 13 virtues."

"In other words, he measured his results against his vision daily."

"Right. And in doing so, he grew acutely aware of what was working and what wasn't. This period of self-examination made him far more conscious and deliberate in his days. By performing this nightly measurement ritual, each day was better than the previous one, and he was able to build a great life."

"Very interesting."

"You see, Jack, there's nothing wrong with making mistakes in life. Mistakes are beautiful teachers. They offer the most fertile ground for personal growth. But there's something wrong with making the same mistakes over and over again throughout our lives. It displays a complete lack of self-awareness and a stubborn refusal to learn from your personal history. The whole idea of the game is to learn from your past. Or maybe a better way to put it is like this: *Let your past serve you.* Leverage the failures of your past into your future wins. If you constantly measure how you're doing against the goals you've set for yourself, then making those all-important course corrections will get you to your best life in no time at all. Which brings me very nicely to the fifth and final step in this model for the fulfillment of your heart's desires."

"I'm all ears, Tess."

"Celebrate your Proud Moments."

"What are they?"

"Proud Moments are those times during your week when you've scored a win in terms of the advancement of the particular desire you're working on. One of the primary reasons we lose our inspiration and passion for making our goals happen is because we spend more time focusing on what's *not* working rather than on what *is*."

"I do that in my life in general," I acknowledged as we walked along a wooded pathway.

"I know you do, Jack, but it's really important to praise progress. Make some time every week to record your Proud Moments. Share them with the members of your mastermind alliance. Engage in a little brag time—it will keep you motivated and energized as you move confidently in the direction of your dream. And this point is really important: Enjoy the ride as you progress toward your goals. Celebrate the tiny successes—they'll fill your heart with excitement and joy over the gifts still to come. As you recognize and appreciate your small wins, enormous momentum will be created that will make you more powerful and even more committed to your ultimate personal dream. Harold Melchert explained it like this: 'Live your life each day as if you would climb mountains. An occasional glance toward the summit puts the goal in mind. Many beautiful scenes can be observed from each new vantage point. Climb steadily, slowly, enjoy each passing moment; and the view from the summit will serve as a fitting climax to the journey.'"

"Beautiful words."

"Yes, they are," Tess agreed. "Jack, speak about your intentions and desires often. Declare them to the world. Tell your family and friends about what you want to have, do, and be. The more you *talk about* what you want, the more you'll *have* what you want."

"Why is that?"

"Because the more you talk about your heart's desires, the higher they'll move into your awareness. You'll begin to see opportunities that were previously invisible. You'll form new connections in your mind and view the possibilities of your life from the highest vantage point."

"Okay. What's next?" I inquired.

"To make this whole process work, you must remember that success lies in its execution," Tess responded.

"In the execution?"

"Yes. The reason why so many business ventures fail is because they're weak in their execution. They haven't built a discipline for getting things done. They might have a brilliant strategy, but they're poor at *implementing* the strategy. Our company is the market leader because we do more than just dream big dreams—we *take* big steps. We're fantastic at getting things done. And I should add that we do more than just get things done—we get the *right* things done. As management guru Peter Drucker once observed: 'There is nothing so useless as doing efficiently that which should not be done at all.'"

"Great point," I said with a smile.

"We're very focused on concentrating on the essentials, those activities that our research has shown will get us to where we've planned to be."

Tess's cell phone rang. "I'm so sorry, Jack," she said, "but I've been expecting this call from Tokyo. Would you mind if I took it?"

"Not at all. Go for it."

She very quickly told the caller she'd call back shortly, and then turned to me. "Jack, I need to get back to the office. We've been working on another public offering, and I must pull our team together to talk strategy."

"And execution," I noted.

"You got it. Anyway, we've gone over everything I've wanted to cover today. Why don't you enjoy this place, and I'll see you tomorrow. You're a great student, and I know you'll do great things. Cal would have been immensely proud of you, Jack. Please know that."

"Thank you, Tess."

—— ✦ ——

After Tess left, I sat under a tree and thought about what she'd taught me. I reflected on the importance of making things happen in life, and tried to reconcile it with Moe's instruction to live in the mystery of it all, staying open to all possibilities.

I realized that success in life came down to a balance. Living in the mystery without being practical and taking steps to plan and then realize one's dreams was nothing more than "spiritual apathy" and a cop-out of sorts. And yet, spending one's days planning, organizing, and focusing was nothing more than trying to control the whole thing. By working and living like this, there's no room for the possibilities that life has to offer to weave themselves into our lives.

Once again, I couldn't fail to notice this fact: Life is all about balance.

15 GATEWAYS TO A BEAUTIFUL LIFE

*"Let everyone sweep in front of their door
and the whole world will be clean."*

— Mother Teresa

———— ✦ ————

The weeks with Tess went by quickly. Like Father Mike and Moe before her, she proved to be not only highly intelligent and unusually creative in terms of her thinking, but she was also a genuinely good person.

Good people really can succeed in business, I realized.

During our weeks together, Tess reinforced the need to be kind and loving in business. She emphasized that relationship building was essential, and that I had to dedicate myself to adding value to others—and to the world at large—if I wanted to manifest my destiny and enjoy authentic success. She told me about the importance of good manners, punctuality, and human decency as strategic advantages, and spoke passionately of the need for every businessperson to show leadership if we ever hoped to improve the state of the world.

As we relaxed in her office one sun-filled afternoon, she

handed me an envelope. I really enjoyed opened it, but was disappointed to find nothing but a crisp, blank sheet of ivory-colored stationery inside.

"I don't get it, Tess. There's nothing written on this paper."

"Jack, today is our final day together. I've just given you a very special gift to thank you for spending these past few weeks with me."

"I still don't understand the significance of this blank piece of paper."

"Later tonight, just before you go to sleep, I'd like you to perform a sacred ritual. Take out this blank sheet and write out the tale of your life on it. Write, as succinctly as possible, how you'd like your life to turn out. Set this intention and capture it on paper. Write about your heart's desires and the difference you hope to make in the world as a result of the person you're becoming. And then, write about your legacy."

"What exactly do you mean by a legacy?"

"The deepest of all human needs is the need to live for something more important than ourselves. Greatness as a human being comes when you dedicate yourself to one thing: living for a cause bigger than yourself. In your silent moments tonight, I'd like you to ask yourself what you want your life to stand for—then write down what the answer is. Contemplate what the footprint you leave behind will look like, and think about how the generations that follow you will remember you. You need to have some kind of a vision and dream about your legacy—believe me, Jack, it will keep you very focused in your days and fill your heart with immense hope."

"Okay, I'll do this exercise tonight."

Tess put her arm around me and kissed me on the cheek. "I have to meet a couple of colleagues downstairs," she said. "Would you mind walking with me?"

"I'd love to. Tess, I've really enjoyed my time with you. You've shared some extraordinary insights that I know will help me in my career and in my life as a whole. Thank you *so* much."

"Anytime, Jack. Just make sure that you pass on all that I've taught you. Be a light in the world, a beacon of wisdom in an uncertain place, a missionary for change and love wherever you go. If you affect the lives of others and are a leader by the way you live your life, then my time with you will have been very well spent indeed."

"Thank you," I said emotionally.

We rode the elevator to the ground floor in silence. I felt we were both sorry to be parting.

As Tess and I walked out onto the bustling street, I saw a bizarre sight. Racing toward us was a bright yellow SUV. The horn was honking, and an old surfboard was strapped to the roof. The vehicle screeched to a halt right in front of us, and I was stunned when I saw who was inside.

It was Moe Jackson and Father Mike.

"Hi, Jack!" they both shouted out in unison, laughing like two little kids at a birthday party.

"You're lookin' great!" exclaimed Moe.

"Wow!" I said. "You two are the last people I would have expected to see in New York City!"

They quickly jumped out of the SUV and gave me a warm hug. Then they turned to Tess.

"Hey, sweetheart," said Moe affectionately. "Ready to roll?"

"Where are you three going?" I asked, burning with curiosity.

"We're having a reunion of sorts, Jack," my surfer friend said. "We're off to celebrate our success. It's kind of a ritual we have every time we do a transformation."

"A transformation?"

"Sure! All three of us worked together to teach you what you needed to learn. Your father was our friend, and we were delighted to work with you. You're a very special human being." Moe paused and looked at me gently. "But, Jack, we've done this before with other people. And we believe *everyone* is special. Every year, a student is sent to us. And every year, we get to share our philosophy and wisdom with yet another person, watching them transform before our very eyes."

"It's the best thing ever!" shouted Father Mike as he revved up the engine like a race-car driver. "When our students succeed, we succeed, too. By helping others grow into their best selves and then go out and impact the world, *we* impact the world."

"That's our legacy," added Tess.

Then, with all three modern-day masters snugly settled into the SUV, they fell silent for a moment.

Finally, Father Mike piped up. "Bless you, Jack."

"Love you, man," said Moe.

"Leave a legacy," instructed Tess.

Moe then reached over and turned on the radio. An old Beach Boys tune blared from the speakers.

"Ah, that's more like it," I heard him say as the SUV started cruising down the road. All three waved to me, grinning and singing along to the radio.

All of a sudden, they stopped. The SUV backed up.

"Oh, I almost forgot. This is for you, Jack. It's something we've all worked on," said Tess as she handed me an elegantly wrapped box. "We hope it will help you along the path of your life. And when you need a little guidance during challenging times, we hope you might think of us and remember these past three months. Life is nothing more than a beautiful adventure, you know. And yours, my friend, has just begun."

With that, the SUV pulled away again, and these three remarkable teachers drove off into the distance, waving to me once again. I thought I was dreaming.

I walked to a nearby park and sat down next to a rosebush. The sunlight warmed my face and the fragrance lifted my spirits. I was feeling sad—my remarkable journey with my three amazing guides had ended, and now I was all alone, left to apply what I'd learned and spread their message in my own unique way. I really wanted to realize who I truly was, and I felt deeply dedicated to living my life according to their philosophies. Most important, I felt the need—as I never had before—to make a difference and do my part to aid in the building of a happier, healthier world.

I reached down and opened up the box. Inside was a leather-bound journal, an exact duplicate of the one Father Mike gave to me on our first day together. I opened it up to the first page. My heart started to race when I read the writing on it. Here's what it said:

GATEWAYS TO A BEAUTIFUL LIFE

#1:   *The main work of every human being is inner work. Each day, do something significant to deepen yourself. To have more of the life that you truly want, you must first become more of who you truly are.*

#2:   *See your life as a fantastic growth school. Everything that you experience, both good and challenging, has come to you to teach you the lesson that you most needed to learn at that particular stage of your evolution as a person. Understand this truth, and keep asking yourself, "What opportunity does this person or situ-*

ation represent" in terms of your personal growth. This is a great source of inner peace.

#3: *Be true to yourself—the best life is the authentic life. Never betray yourself. Take off your social mask and have the personal bravery to present the real you to the world. The world will be richer for it.*

#4: *Remember that we collect what we project. Our outer lives are nothing more than a mirror image of our inner lives. Pour light on your dark side. Become aware of the false assumptions, limiting beliefs, and fears that are keeping you small, and your exterior world will change.*

#5: *We see the world not as it is but as we are. Know that the truth in any given circumstance is filtered through your personal stained glass window—your personal context. Clean up the windows, and you'll clean up your life. Then you'll see the truth.*

#6: *Live in your heart—its wisdom never lies. Follow the quiet promptings of your heart, and you'll be led in the direction of your destiny.*

#7: *Stand in the curiosity of your life. In surrendering control, you'll create a space for possibilities to enter and treasures to flow.*

#8: *Care for yourself. Do something each day to nurture your mind, body, and spirit. These are essential acts of self-respect and self-love.*

#9: *Build human connections. Dedicate yourself to deepening your bonds with the people around you. Focus on helping others achieve their dreams, and be more concerned with selfless service rather than self-gratification. You're here to enrich this world, and you betray yourself once you forget this truth.*

#10:   *Leave a legacy. The deepest longing of the human heart is the need to live for a cause greater than oneself.*

I closed my eyes and absorbed the wisdom I'd just read. An immense feeling of peace, and then utter joy, washed over me. I felt so grateful for this moment and sat fully within it.

Then I put down the journal and stood up, reaching my hands toward the sky. It was a glorious day to be alive.

THE SHARMA LEADERSHIP REPORT™

FREE subscription offer to purchasers of
The Saint, the Surfer, and the CEO for a limited
time only. (Annual subscription has a
$95 value.)

The *Sharma Leadership Report,* Robin
Sharma's popular newsletter, is packed with
practical wisdom, lessons, and tips that you
can apply immediately to improve the
quality of your life. This highly inspirational
report focuses on leading-edge topics for
personal, professional, and character development including self-esteem, inner renwal,
life-career balance, relationships, self-leadership, stress mastery,
and career leadership.

To order your free subscription, simply visit
www.robinsharma.com and register online today.

KEYNOTES & SEMINARS
WITH ROBIN SHARMA
Bestselling Author & Professional Speaker

Robin Sharma is one of North America's most thought-provoking
and electrifying professional speakers. His powerful wisdom and pio-
neering insights on leadership, managing rapid change, personal
effectiveness, and life renewal have made him the first choice of
organizations seeking a high-profile keynote speaker or seminar leader
whose message will transform lives and restore commitment in these
turbulent times. Robin Sharma's enormously inspirational presenta-
tions are fully customized through a unique research process, rich in
practical content and designed to help your people rise to all-new
levels of perfromance, passion, creativity, and personal fulfillment.

To book Robin for your next conference or in-house seminar,
visit **www.robinsharma.com** or call:

Marnie Ballane
V.P. of Speaking Services
Sharma Leadership International
Telephone: 1-888-RSHARMA (774-2762)
e-mail: marnie@robinsharma.com

PERSONAL COACHING
WITH ROBIN SHARMA

1. THE MONTHLY COACH™

The Monthly Coach is Robin's highly acclaimed book- and CD-of-the-month club. Each month, you receive one of the most powerful books available on personal development and self-discovery, along with a CD recording of Robin's summary of the book's best points and his insights on how to translate the book's knowledge into real results in your life. This program is life changing.

2. THE ROBIN SHARMA LIFE COACHING PROCESS™

This is Robin's revolutionary system for people who are ready to create extraordinary lives. You meet with Robin in a small group setting every three months over the course of a year to experience one of the most effective programs for personal transformation and self-renewal available today. Also available in a three-day format.

3. THE ELITE PERFORMERS SERIES™

The Elite Performers Series is Sharma Leadership International's flagship corporate coaching program, which is designed to transform employees into leaders who excel amid change. Presented by Robin to your organization's employees over four incredible days, The Elite Performers Series will inspire your team to operate at all-new levels of effectiveness, excellence, and personal responsibility.

4. THE MASTERS SERIES

This is an exclusive program for executives and entrepreneurs seeking world-class, one-on-one coaching to create extraordinary results both professionally and personally. You meet weekly with one of our Lead Coaches via telephone or the Internet and experience a powerful process that has helped thousands of people transform the way they think, feel, and act. Robin Sharma himself accepts up to five executive coaching clients each year to serve as their personal life coach.

For more information on these personal coaching options, please contact our Vice-President of Coaching Services, Al Moscardelli, at:

Sharma Leadership International
Toll-free: 1-888-RSHARMA (774-2762)
e-mail: coaching@robinsharma.com
Website: **www.robinsharma.com**

POWERFUL WISDOM FOR LEADERSHIP
AND IN BUSINESS AND IN LIFE

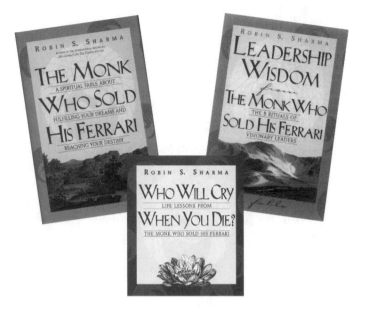

NOW AVAILABLE IN ALL GOOD BOOKSTORES

Discounts available on quantity purchases for your
organization. Please call **1-888-RSHARMA**
or e-mail: **info@robinsharma.com** for pricing information.

ABOUT ROBIN SHARMA

Robin Sharma is one of the world's premier thinkers on leadership in business and in life. He is the author of numerous books, including the #1 international bestseller *The Monk Who Sold His Ferrari;* its bestselling sequel *Leadership Wisdom from The Monk Who Sold His Ferrari; Family Wisdom from The Monk Who Sold His Ferrari;* and *Begin Within.* Sharma is also in constant demand across the globe as a keynote speaker for organizations dedicated to developing leaders at all levels. Clients include Fortune 500 companies such as Microsoft, General Motors, IBM, FedEx, and Nortel Networks, as well as leading trade associations.

A former lawyer who holds two law degrees, including a master's of law, Robin Sharma is the CEO of Sharma Leadership International (SLI), a widely respected training firm that offers a range of services and products to help employees realize their highest potential for extraordinary professional and personal results amidst relentless change. SLI also runs the highly acclaimed *Robin Sharma Life Coaching Program*™, a strikingly effective coaching process that shows individuals and corporate teams how to create the personal lives they want while becoming a star at work. Sharma Leadership International also offers *The Monthly Coach* program—the acclaimed book/CD-of-the-month club where Robin personally selects a life-changing work that will enhance your growth and enrich your life. He will send it to you every 30 days for continual improvement.

For more information on any of these services or to see our complete line of learning products, please visit **www.robinsharma.com** or call **1-888-RSHARMA.**

OTHER HAY HOUSE TITLES
OF RELATED INTEREST

Books

The Breakthrough Experience:
A Revolutionary New Approach to Personal Transformation,
by Dr. John F. Demartini

Gratitude: *A Way of Life,*
by Louise L. Hay and Friends

Inner Peace for Busy People:
52 Simple Strategies for Transforming Your Life,
by Joan Borysenko, Ph.D.

Wisdom of the Heart:
Inspiration for a Life Worth Living, by Alan Cohen

Audio Programs

**How to Get What You
Really, Really, Really, Really Want,**
by Dr. Wayne W. Dyer and Deepak Chopra, M.D.

Self-Coaching Secrets for Success,
a Dialogue Between Tom Gegax and Deepak Chopra, M.D.

Tools for Success:
Learning to Change Your Thoughts and Change Your Life,
by Louise L. Hay

———— ✦ ————

We hope you enjoyed this Hay House book. If you
would like to receive a free catalog featuring additional
Hay House books and products, or if you would like information about the Hay Foundation, please contact:

Hay House, Inc.
P.O. Box 5100
Carlsbad, CA 92018-5100

(760) 431-7695 or **(800) 654-5126**
(760) 431-6948 (fax) or **(800) 650-5115 (fax)**
www.hayhouse.com

———— ✦ ————

Published and distributed in Australia by:
Hay House Australia Pty Ltd, P.O. Box 515,
Brighton-Le-Sands, NSW 2216 • *phone:* 1800 023 516
e-mail: info@hayhouse.com.au

Distributed in the United Kingdom by: Airlift,
8 The Arena, Mollison Ave., Enfield, Middlesex,
United Kingdom EN3 7NL

Distributed in Canada by: Raincoast, 9050 Shaughnessy St.,
Vancouver, B.C., Canada V6P 6E5
e-mail: info@hayhouse.com.au

———— ✦ ————

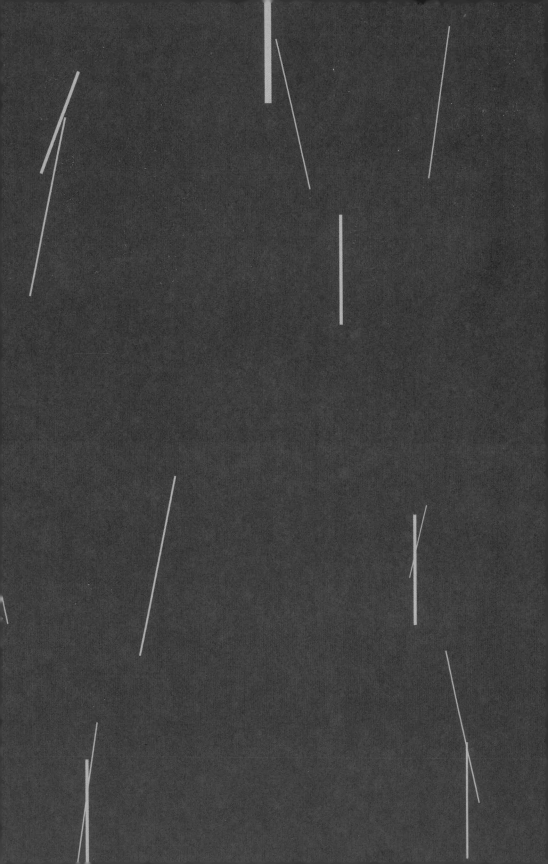